THE GREAT AMERICAN THINKERS SERIES

D1211320

This new series of original works is designed to present in highly readable form the flow of American thought from colonial times to the present. Each volume has been written by a leading scholar and is devoted to a single man in the history of American thought who represents a particular trend or movement within the great span of our culture. Each book in the series contains a short biography of the man, a critical evaluation of his central ideas and their influence upon American thought as a whole, as well as an extensive bibliography and an index.

The Great American Thinkers Series is designed for the general reader as well as the serious college student or higher-level secondary school student, and is under the general editorship of two distinguished American educators: Thomas S. Knight, Ph.D., Professor of Philosophy and Chairman, Department of Philosophy, Ontario College of Education, University of Western Ontario; and Arthur W. Brown, Ph.D., President of Adelphi University. WILLIAM JAMES was written by Edward Carter Moore, Ph.D., Graduate Dean and Coordinator of Research, University of Massachusetts. Dean Moore has written extensively on William James and other American Pragmatists.

THE GREAT AMERICAN THINKERS SERIES

JONATHAN EDWARDS, by Alfred Owen Aldridge, Ph.D., Professor of English and Director of the Program of Comparative Literature, University of Maryland.

BENJAMIN FRANKLIN, by Ralph L. Ketcham, Ph.D., Associate Editor of the *Papers of Benjamin Franklin*, Yale University, and Professor of American Studies, Syracuse University.

JOHN WOOLMAN, by Edwin H. Cady, Ph.D., Rudy Professor of English, University of Indiana.

THOMAS JEFFERSON, by Stuart Gerry Brown, Ph.D., Maxwell Professor of American Civilization, Syracuse University.

ALEXANDER HAMILTON, by Stuart Gerry Brown, Ph.D., Maxwell Professor of American Civilization, Syracuse University.

JOHN C. CALHOUN, by Richard N. Current, Ph.D., Professor of History, University of Wisconsin.

GEORGE BANCROFT, by Russel B. Nye, Ph.D., Professor of English, Michigan State University.

THEODORE PARKER, by Arthur W. Brown, Ph.D., Director of the Institute of Humanities and Chairman of the English Department, Adelphi University.

CHAUNCEY WRIGHT, by Edward Madden, Ph.D., Professor of Philosophy, State University of New York at Buffalo.

CHARLES PEIRCE, by Thomas S. Knight, Ph.D., Professor of Philosophy and Chairman, Department of Philosophy, Ontario College of Education, University of Western Ontario.

WILLIAM JAMES, by Edward C. Moore, Ph.D., Graduate Dean and Coordinator of Research, University of Massachusetts.

THORSTEIN VEBLEN, by Douglas Dowd, Ph.D., Professor of Economics, Cornell University.

JOHN DEWEY, by Richard J. Bernstein, Ph.D., Associate Professor of Philosophy, Yale University, and Assistant Editor of *Review of Metaphysics*.

DR. W. E. B. DuBOIS, by Henry Lee Moon, Director of Public Relations, National Association for the Advancement of Colored People.

NORMAN THOMAS, by Robert J. Alexander, Ph.D., Professor of Economics, Rutgers University.

WILLIAM JAMES

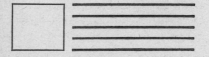

Author of this volume: Edward
Carter Moore, Graduate Dean and
Coordinator of Research, Univer-
sity of Massachusetts.

Series Editors: Thomas S. Knight,
Ph.D., Professor of Philosophy and
Chairman, Department of Philoso-
phy, Ontario College of Education,
University of Western Ontario;
and Arthur W. Brown, Ph.D.,
President of Adelphi University.

WASHINGTON SQUARE PRESS, INC. • NEW YORK

WILLIAM JAMES

A *Washington Square Press* edition
1st printing......................February, 1965

L

Published by
Washington Square Press, Inc., 630 Fifth Avenue, New York, N.Y.

WASHINGTON SQUARE PRESS editions are distributed in
the U.S. by Affiliated Publishers, a division of Pocket
Books, Inc., 630 Fifth Avenue, New York 20, N.Y.

PREFACE

Perhaps it is the fate of philosophers to be misunderstood. It is at any rate true that a careful examination of their writings often seems to suggest a rather different picture than is found in common opinions of their thought. To this rule Williams James is no exception. He is best known for one or two ideas expressed in an essay here or a chapter there. Taken out of the context of his whole work, his essay on "The Will to Believe" and his pragmatic theory of truth have often resulted in a considerably distorted view of his philosophy.

The present volume is intended to help correct these misapprehensions by giving appropriate emphasis to the various elements of James's thought, so that the more notorious ones do not take an undue share of the spotlight. I have tried to present these various aspects in such a way that early in the discussion of each problem an elementary analysis of it is made. Hopefully this will allow the reader who has little training in philosophy to pick up the thread of the discussion before it moves on into the more rarefied atmosphere that philosophers customarily breathe.

William James enjoyed philosophy. He pursued it with

a gusto that approached passion. As I reread his works during the writing of this book some of this excitement was passed on to me. I hope that whether the reader is persuaded or not by James's views, he will at least sense some of the excitement of philosophy. Philosophers sometimes forget what James never forgot—that the root meaning of "philosopher" is not "possessor of wisdom" but "lover of wisdom."

EDWARD C. MOORE

UNIVERSITY OF MASSACHUSETTS
AMHERST, MASSACHUSETTS
November 1, 1963

TABLE OF CONTENTS

WILLIAM JAMES

Philosophies are intimate parts of the universe, they express something of its own thought of itself. It may, as I said, possess and handle itself differently in consequence of us philosophers, with our theories, being here; it may trust itself or mistrust itself the more, and, by doing the one or the other, deserve more the trust or mistrust. What mistrusts itself deserves mistrust.

—William James

Chapter 1

RELIGION: MAN AND GOD

Perhaps no American thinker has so endeared himself to his fellow countrymen as has William James. The reasons for this are not hard to find. James embodied in his own intellectual development and in his personal emotional concerns the primary philosophical and spiritual struggles which have haunted Americans since the first colonists landed in New England. These struggles are by no means over, nor have they lost their interest. The intellectual biography of William James is almost an intellectual biography of America. To understand the problems which James coped with intellectually and to respond perceptively to the solutions which he arrived at is to understand the inner life of more individual Americans than would be the case if one studied any other representative thinker.

It is seldom noted that the landing of the Puritans in Massachusetts was contemporaneous with the discovery by Kepler and Galileo of evidence substantiating the Copernican theory of the solar system. The landing of the Pilgrims and the verification of the heliocentric theory were events which, while separated greatly in space, were to approach one another with increasing relevance as time ran on. The stage was being set for what came to be called variously the struggle or the conflict or even the warfare between science and religion. The New England Puritans represented the theological momentum of a long effort, ranging from St. Augustine to Calvin, to gain insight into the supernatural dimensions of the human situation. On the other hand, Kepler and Galileo were the harbingers of an increasingly powerful effort continuing through Newton and Darwin to understand the human predicament in more natural terms.

Whenever, in the long history of mankind, theology and science have found themselves at odds, they have made philosophy the middleman to whom they have appealed for mediation. When Protestant supernaturalism met the new scientific naturalism on the stage of American thought at the end of the nineteenth century, one of the chief protagonists was to be the philosopher William James.

No true statement can convey more misinformation about William James than the statement that he was born in New York City on January 11, 1842. James was not a New Yorker but a New Englander. Although he knew Europe as few Americans did and became cosmopolitan in his interests and friendships, he never became the worldly sophisticate purportedly typified by the term "New Yorker." He persevered all his life long, until the day of his death in Chocorua, New Hampshire, on August 26, 1910, in maintaining a constant and pervasive concern for the inner life of man as contrasted with the trappings of outward existence. In this fundamental sense he was the perpetual New Englander. Nor would it be significantly correct to say that he was born in 1842. His intellectual concerns, at least, were born centuries before as ideas in the minds of Plato and Aristotle and St. Augustine and Luther and Calvin. Although these ideas attained a physical incarceration in the body of William

James, they neither began with his birth nor ended with his death.

James possessed to an exceptional degree the one trait of primary significance to the philosophical pursuit: he knew a genuine philosophical problem when he saw one. It is not an uncommon sight to see philosophers who go off in all directions in pursuit of problems which careful examination shows to be the mere appearance of problems. To have the true nose for the real issues is to be able to make the hunt of overriding interest, to keep us on the trail of those problems which are of fundamental concern. To ride with James is to track down the great problems of Western man. Although the answers almost invariably evade the most subtle of our efforts, the interest occasioned by the problems suffices to prove again the truth of the proverb that the hunt is more exhilarating than the capture. To get truly on the scent of the problems James presents for our consideration is to attain a short course in the great and perennial questions of philosophical concern. James's intellectual life is well typified by the title of the book upon which he was working at the time of his death: *Some Problems in Philosophy*. To study the life of William James is to study some problems in philosophy—problems which focus on the relations of science to man. Certainly these problems are of no less concern in the age of the atom bomb than they were in James's own day.

The James family came to this country in the person of another William James, the grandfather of our philosopher. William James the elder came as an immigrant from Ireland in 1789 at the age of eighteen. He arrived here with little money but great ambition. He settled in Albany, New York, where he pursued successively and successfully the tobacco business, an express business between Albany and Utica, and extensive holdings in real estate. He made judicious investments in the Erie Canal and died leaving to his children an estate worth three million dollars. In his will he not only provided for the economic well-being of his children and grand-children, but he sought to tie them to him also in his religious concerns. His will provided for their sharing his wealth only if they shared his piety. This latter scheme failed of any legal force, but the concern with Calvinism and Presbyterianism nevertheless produced an atmosphere which was to color the intellectual and emotional concerns of his son, Henry James the elder, who was, in turn, to be the father of William James, the philosopher, and Henry James, Jr., the novelist.

Calvinism was not a position to which either Henry James the elder or William James was to adhere. They were not New Englanders in that sense. But it was a position they were to react against and with which they had, each in his own way, to make peace.

Henry James the elder is one of the more neglected figures in American intellectual history. Bernard Shaw once sought to shock Henry James, Jr., by remarking that the most interesting member of the family was neither Henry, the novelist, nor William, the philosopher, but their father, Henry, Sr. From this view Henry, Jr., did not dissent. The reader of the writings of Henry, Sr., can discern in them both a literary and an intellectual quality of a high order. It is clear to one who reads both Henry, Sr., and William that the former is the source of much of the literary felicity of the latter. It also becomes increasingly clear that the problems with which William struggled the most vigorously during his period of intellectual maturity were the problems he shared with his father and which it may even be said he inherited from him.

When William James wrote to his sister, Alice, that

"Religion is the great interest of my life,"[1] he was expressing a sentiment that was almost a family tradition. It
is difficult to convey to a modern reader the emotional
weight of a religious upbringing in the rigorous Calvinism of New England in the nineteenth century. The following selections from the autobiography of Henry James
the elder may convey some sense of the emotionally
loaded atmosphere:

The aim of all formal religious worship, as it stood
impressed upon my youthful imagination, was to
save the soul of the worshipper from a certain
liability to Divine wrath which he had incurred as
the inheritor of a fallen nature, and from which he
could only get relief through the merits of Christ
imputed to him, and apprehended by faith. I had
been traditionally taught, and I traditionally took
for granted, that all souls had originally forfeited
the creative good will in the person of Adam, their
attorney or representative, even if they should never
have aggravated that catastrophe subsequently in
their own persons; so that practically every man or
woman born comes into the world charged with a
weight of Divine obstruction or limitation utterly
hopeless and crushing, unless relieved by actual faith
in the atoning blood of Christ. I ought not to say
that I actually believed this puerile and disgusting
caricature of the gospel, for one believes only with
the heart, and my heart at all events inmostly loathed
this dogmatic fouling of the creative name, even
while it passively endured its authoritative imposi-
tion.[2]

. . . I began very early to discover disorderly ten-
dencies, or prove rebellious to religious restraints.

I cannot imagine anything more damaging to the infant mind than to desecrate its natural delights, or impose upon it an ascetic regimen. For nature is eternal in all her subjects, and when the child's natural instincts are violently suppressed or driven inwards by some overpowering outward authority, a moral feverishness is sure to result, which would finally exhaust or consume every possibility of his future manhood, if nature did not incontinently put him to seeking a clandestine satisfaction of her will. I felt this impulse very strongly; I doubt whether ever any one more so. I had always had the keenest savor and relish of whatsoever came to me by nature's frank inspiration or free gift. The common ore of existence perpetually converted itself into the gold of life in the glowing fire of my animal spirits. I lived in every fibre of my body. The dawn always found me on my feet; and I can still vividly recall the divine rapture which filled my blood as I pursued under the magical light of morning the sports of the river, the wood, or the field. And here was a law which frowned—nay, scowled—upon that jocund unconscious existence; which drew a pall over the lovely outlying world of sense, and gave me to feel that I pursued its pleasures only at the imminent risk of immortal loss. Just conceive the horror of leading the tender mind of childhood to believe that the Divine being could under any circumstance grudge it its natural delights; could care, for example, for the holiness of any stupid day of the seven in comparison with the holiness of its innocent mind and body! Herod's politic slaughter of the innocents were mercy itself beside this wanton outrage to nature.

The thought of God as a power foreign to my nature, and with interests therefore hostile to my own, would have wilted my manhood in its cradle, would have made a thoughtful, anxious, and weary little slave of me before I had entered upon my teens, if it had not been for Nature's indomitable uprightness. It aroused a reflective self-consciousness in me when I ought by natural right to have been wholly immersed in my senses, and known nothing but the innocent pleasures and salutary pains they impart. I doubt whether any lad had ever just so thorough and pervading a belief in God's existence as an outside and contrarious force to humanity, as I had. The conviction of his supernatural being and attributes was burnt into me as with a red-hot iron, and I am sure no childish sinews were ever more strained than mine were in wrestling with the subtle terror of his name. This insane terror pervaded my consciousness more or less. It turned every hour of unallowed pleasure I enjoyed into an actual boon wrung from his forbearance; made me loath at night to lose myself in sleep, lest his dread hand should clip my thread of life without time for a parting sob of penitence, and grovel at morning dawn with an abject slavish gratitude that the sweet sights and sounds of Nature and of man were still around me. The terror was all but overpowering.[3]

Several generations of the James family felt the weight of the Calvinist tradition. It did not sit well on their Irish temperament. The steeping of an outgoing Irish *joie de vivre* in a dour Calvinistic puritanism was not a happy arrangement. We have records of serious psychic neuroses occasioned by religious conflict in three of the first four generations of the James family in this country.

We can bring our problem into focus and into William James's own life by recounting these reports.

Henry James the elder records the following concerning his maternal grandmother:

. . . It was not till I had grown up, and she herself was among the blessed, that I discovered that she had undergone a great deal of mental suffering, and dimly associated this fact somehow with the great conscience she had always made of us children. She had been from youth a very religious person, without a shadow of scepticism or indifference in her mental temperament; but as life matured and her heart became mellowed under its discipline, she fell to doubting whether the dogmatic traditions in which she had been bred effectively represented Divine truth. And the conflict grew so active erelong between this quickened allegiance of her heart to God, and the merely habitual deference her intellect was under to men's opinions, as to allow her afterwards no fixed rest this side of the grave. In her most depressed condition, however, she maintained an equable front before the world, fulfilled all her duties to her family and her neighborhood, and yielded at last to death, as I afterwards learned, in smiling confidence of a speedy resolution of all her doubts. . . . Nor could I doubt when in after years my own hour of tribulation sounded, and I too felt my first immortal longing "to bathe myself in innocency," that this dear old lady had found in the ignorance and innocence of the grandchildren whom she loved to hug to her bosom a truer gospel balm, a far more soothing and satisfactory echo of Divine knowledge, than she had ever caught from the logic of John Calvin.[4]

Henry James the elder had his own hour of tribulation when he was thirty-three. He had been working for several years on a study of the Book of Genesis. He tells us that he was cheerful and in good spirits when he had the following experience:

One day, however, towards the close of May, having eaten a comfortable dinner, I remained sitting at the table after the family had dispersed, idly gazing at the embers in the grate, thinking of nothing, and feeling only the exhilaration incident to a good digestion, when suddenly—in a lightning flash as it were—"fear came upon me, and trembling, which made all my bones shake." To all appearance it was a perfectly insane and abject terror, without ostensible cause, and only to be accounted for, to my perplexed imagination, by some damned shape squatting invisible to me within the precincts of the room and raying out from his fetid personality influences fatal to life. The thing had not lasted ten seconds before I felt myself a wreck; that is, reduced from a state of firm, vigorous, joyful manhood to one of almost helpless infancy. The only self-control I was capable of exerting was to keep my seat. I felt the greatest desire to run incontinently to the foot of the stairs and shout for help to my wife, to run to the roadside even, and appeal to the public to protect me; but by an immense effort I controlled these frenzied impulses, and determined not to budge from my chair till I had recovered my lost self-possession. This purpose I held to for a good long hour, as I reckoned time, beat upon meanwhile by an ever-growing tempest of doubt, anxiety, and despair, with absolutely no relief from any truth I had ever encountered save a most pale and distant glimmer of the divine existence, when I resolved to abandon the vain struggle, and communicate without more ado what seemed my sudden burden of inmost, implacable unrest to my wife.

Now, to make a long story short, this ghastly condition of mind continued with me, with gradually lengthening intervals of relief, for two years, and even longer.[5]

William James the younger had an experience of about the same sort when he was in his thirties. He was studying abroad on his medical degree. He has described his experience in these words:

I went one evening into a dressing-room in the twilight to procure some article that was there, when suddenly there fell upon me without any warning, just as if it came out of the darkness, a horrible fear of my own existence. Simultaneously there arose in my mind the image of an epileptic patient whom I had seen in the asylum, a black-haired youth with greenish skin, entirely idiotic, who used to sit all day on one of the benches, or rather shelves against the wall, with his knees drawn up against his chin, and the coarse gray undershirt, which was his only garment, drawn over them inclosing his entire figure. He sat there like a sort of sculptured Egyptian cat or Peruvian mummy, moving nothing but his black eyes and looking absolutely non-human. This image and my fear entered into a species of combination with each other. *That shape am I,* I felt potentially. Nothing that I possess can defend me against that fate, if the hour for it should strike for me as it struck for him. There was such a horror of him, and such a perception of my own merely momentary discrepancy from him, that it was as if something hitherto solid within my breast gave way entirely, and I became a mass of quivering fear. After this the universe was changed for me altogether. I awoke morning after morning with a horrible dread at the pit of my stomach, and with a sense of the insecurity of life that I never knew before, and that I have never felt since. It was like a revelation; and although the immediate feelings passed away, the experience has made me sympathetic with the morbid feelings of others ever since. It gradually faded, but for months I was unable to go out into the dark alone.

In general I dreaded to be left alone. I remember wondering how other people could live, how I myself had ever lived, so unconscious of that pit of insecurity beneath the surface of life. . . . I have always thought that this experience of melancholia of mine had a religious bearing.[6]

The problems suggested by this religious difficulty remained with James throughout his entire life. His early education was an unusual one. His father had his own ideas about the education of his children, and they attended first one school and then another. During the period when William was thirteen to eighteen years of age, the children attended school abroad. During these years James acquired a cosmopolitan touch and a fluency in French and German which were to remain with him all his life and provide him with an acquaintanceship with European intellectuals which made him one of the first Americans widely known in Europe.

James went through a period when he thought he was to be a painter but eventually gave that up. He attended the Lawrence Scientific School at Harvard and in 1864 entered the Harvard Medical School. He studied there under Louis Agassiz and in 1865-66 accompanied Agassiz on an expedition up the Amazon. After this expedition he took up his studies in Europe and in 1869 received his M. D. from Harvard. In 1878 he became an instructor in anatomy and physiology at Harvard and in 1880 became an assistant professor of philosophy. In 1890 he published his two-volume study *The Principles of Psychology,* which long remained the standard work in this country on that subject.

After the publication of this book his interests switched more directly to philosophy, and in 1896 he completed his first collection of philosophical writings, *The Will to Believe and Other Essays.* In 1901 and 1902 he gave the Gifford Lectures at Edinburgh, which were published in 1902 as *The Varieties of Religious Experience.* In 1907 he published *Pragmatism,* which grew out of a series of lectures given the previous year. In 1909 he published *A Pluralistic Universe,* the Hibbert Lectures given at Oxford in 1908 and 1909; also in 1909 he published *The Meaning of Truth.* Posthumous publications were *Some Problems of Philosophy,* 1911; *Memories and Studies,* 1911; *Essays in Radical Empiricism,* 1912; and *Collected Essays and Reviews,* 1920. Extensive biographical information about William James is available primarily in the classic two-volume study done by one of his students, Ralph Barton Perry, in 1935, titled *The Thought and Character of William James,* and in the collection *The Letters of William James,* edited by his son Henry James.

What William James sought for in all of his philosophizing about religion was a middle way between what he envisioned as two extremes. He is constantly establishing dichotomies and then seeking to resolve them. We are told of the tough-minded man versus the tender-minded one, of the "tenderfoot Bostonian" versus "the Rocky Mountain tough," of the "healthy-minded soul" and the "sick soul."

The dichotomy which James was wrestling with fundamentally in all of these problems was the dichotomy between the position of the supernaturalist in religion and that of the naturalist. To state each of these positions briefly, supernaturalism is the view that there is something more than what we find in the natural world—a "super" nature, something "over" nature or "above" or "beyond" the natural world of time and place. This something more is some being (or beings) to whom the natural categories of time and space do not apply. This being has no beginning in time and no end; it is not to be located at some point in space such that if we went to that point we would find it. It is literally outside of time and space. This supernatural being is important in the creation and history of the world. It has some overarching cosmic purpose which permeates the whole scheme of things, so that what is ultimate in the universe is not your purpose in life or my purpose but a cosmic purpose which gives meaning to all things. A usual corollary of supernaturalism is the notion that some part of the supernatural is embodied in man—a soul—which participates in the supernatural and is in some sense timeless or immortal. Supernaturalisms vary greatly as to the details of these doctrines.

Naturalism, which is the contrary view to supernaturalism, holds that all that exists, exists in time and in space. The naturalist denies the existence of any "supernatural" being and thus necessarily of any cosmic purpose or any immortal human soul.

The contrast between these two views is sharp indeed. Historically the efforts to establish the dominance of one or the other have often been carried on through the medium of philosophical argument. Philosophical arguments have not always done very well in the long haul of history. We may examine some of the traditional arguments briefly to see why James does not depend upon them to settle this problem.

There are a number of traditional arguments intended to "prove" the existence of a supernatural being. The only two still taken very seriously by James's day were the so-called Argument from Design and the First Cause Argument.

The Argument from Design goes something like this: There is design exhibited in the natural world. For example, the eye is sensitive to light waves of a certain frequency and the physical world is designed to emit light waves of the required frequency. This evidence of design can be found in great detail and infinite complexity in the natural world. To use a simple illustration of the detailed treatment, a woodpecker must be well designed. His bill must be strong to stand up under the hammering he gives it. It must be firmly embedded in a skull of great strength or the transmitting of the force to the skull would result in brain concussion. He must have strong back muscles to impart the force for the hammer blows of the head. He must have strong claws to provide a firm grasp on the tree trunk. His tail, which provides a fulcrum against which the leverage of back muscles is operative, must be designed for its job. His stomach must be able to extract nourishment from insects ingested as a result of all this process, etc., etc. If the woodpecker were poorly designed in any one of these important respects he would not be able to succeed as a woodpecker. The infinite care and patience exhibited in the design of the woodpecker can be demonstrated over and over again in manifold detail in the whole of nature. Recognizing this evidence of design in nature we are impelled to ask ourselves: who is the designer? Where there is design there must be a designer. All this multifarious fitting of ends to means could not have occurred by chance, there must be a designer, and this designer is God.

So goes the Argument from Design. This was the argument upon which rested the primary weight for the proof of God's existence at the middle of the nineteenth century. This was the argument which the theory of evolution undercut so completely, and this was a primary source of the controversy concerning that theory. For if the theory of evolution was true, the Argument from Design was eliminated as proof of the existence of a supernatural being. The Argument from Design had come under attack in the eighteenth century from David Hume and Immanuel Kant, who pointed out that even if successful, the argument only demonstrated the existence of a designer—what Kant called a Divine Architect—it did not suffice to prove that the designer was beneficent rather than malevolent, or that he was in fact supernatural rather than natural. The argument established no divine Providence which would answer prayers or concern itself with human welfare and woe.

Darwinism cut even deeper. It said that the so-called evidence of design was simply the result of two natural forces operative in the biological realm. The first of these was random variation—sporting or mutation—the coming into existence of new species, by what in Darwin's day seemed to be chance processes but which we have causal explanations for today. The second was the process of natural selection—what Huxley dubbed "the survival of the fittest"—a natural screening process which eliminated the poorly designed among the mutant species and thus left as visible evidence only the well-designed. The woodpeckers whose bills had the consistency of soda crackers either died out or became canaries. They did not survive as woodpeckers.

This rebuttal to the Argument from Design was at least as old as the ancient Greeks. The force of Darwinism, however, was that it brought to the arena biologically detailed evidence substantiating the rebuttal with empirically observed data. This was not Darwin's intent. He was merely concerned with establishing a biological theory. But the result of establishing the theory was the undercutting of the Argument from Design. William James was by training a physiologist and his degree was an M. D. He knew the strength of the evidence for Darwin's theory. As the evidence accumulated, the problem of how to provide a meaningful base for a belief in supernaturalism became increasingly acute for him and his generation.

In addition to the Argument from Design there was the First Cause Argument for the existence of God. The First Cause Argument was intended to answer the question: where did everything come from? What caused it? The argument was based on a regress of causation. For example, if asked what caused the state of the world today—call this A—one might reply that the state of the world today, A, was caused by the state of the world yesterday, say B, so that B caused A. But an insistent inquirer might persevere: "What caused the state of the world yesterday?" To which the reply might be given: "The state of the world the day before yesterday, C. C caused B." "But what caused C?" "D!" "What caused D?" "E!" and so the answers continue to regress. Now, the First Cause Argument is that there cannot be an infinite regression of causes. An infinite regression has no beginning; so if there were an infinite regression there would be no beginning of the causal sequence, and if there were no beginning it would never have begun, and if it never had begun it would not be here—but this is a *reductio ad absurdum,* for it is here, therefore it must have begun, therefore it must have had a beginning, therefore it is not an infinite regress and therefore there must have been a first cause in the series of causes. This first cause which causes all other causes has no cause preceding it and hence is itself uncaused. It is the Uncaused Cause of Aristotle, the First Cause or Prime Mover of all things.

This argument, which has a good deal of plausibility because of its logical intricacy and continuity, is not so plausible if one cuts through the persiflage. If we ask where the Uncaused Cause comes from we are told that this is a mystery beyond human comprehension. When we began our inquiry into where everything came from we were seeking to explain a mystery. We are told that the only answer to our mystery is another mystery. But a mystery is no answer; it leaves our question unanswered. In fact there is no point to producing a long chain of argument designed to explain a mystery by producing another mystery, since this only duplicates the mysteries. We are better off to simply take our universe as a brute, unexplained mystery and let it go at that. The First Cause Argument neither explains where everything comes from nor proves the existence of God. It only makes a confusion so intricate as to give us an emotional feeling of having reached a resting point, when in fact we have failed to do so.

The reader who has followed the above discussion will now have some sense of the state of mind of many persons of William James's generation. Darwin published *The Origin of Species* in 1859. William James, born in 1842, was raised in the pre-Darwinian, supernaturalistic, Calvinistic, New England atmosphere. His father's writings although anti-Calvin were strongly supernatural—the elder James considered himself a follower of Swedenborg, the Swedish mystic. From this atmosphere the transition into Darwinism was abrupt and emotionally disturbing. James could not bring himself to give up his supernaturalism, nor could he bring himself to deny the scientific evidences of his empirical laboratory experiences.

The particular problem which brought so much of this into focus for James was the problem of evil. This was also an old problem. Going back at least to the book of Job, it was a problem to which James's father had addressed himself at some length.

The problem of evil developed because the philosophical naturalists in attacking the position of the supernaturalists were not content with simply pointing out weaknesses in the arguments of their opponents. They had a strong argument of their own, which rested on the problem of evil.

The name of this problem is confusing. In its basic sense it is not concerned with moral evil or what might be called human evil. It does not ask as to why men kill or rob or lie to one another. The presumed answer to this is that there is a weakness in man and this is the reason he does evil. This evil is caused by him. The "problem of evil" is the larger problem of why there is non-man-caused evil in the world. The argument usually assumes that physical pain is an evil thing and that premature death is an evil thing. It asks then why there is non-man-caused pain and premature death in the world. Why are there disease germs (which man does not create)? Why are there tornadoes and tidal waves, which man does not cause and cannot control, which take human lives? Why do these ills fall upon the guilty and the innocent alike? Who causes them and to what end? If there is a designer to the universe he must have designed the ill as well as the good. Since there is a great deal of human ill and suffering over which man has no control, this would cast serious doubts on the Argument from Design and the beneficence of the designer.

This difficulty is particularly acute for a form of supernaturalism—such as Calvinism—which requires that the supernatural being is omnipotent, for if there exists an omnipotent being he would be able to eliminate such evils and if he were good he would want to eliminate them, but they are not eliminated since we have them. We are left with four alternatives: (1) We can hold that no supernatural being exists and therefore there is no problem of explaining evil as a contradiction of divine benevolence. This is the path the naturalist pursues. (2) We can hold that this being is not omnipotent, so that although he would like to eliminate the evil he cannot; this is the path of Plato, for example. (3) We can hold that God's goodness is of a different kind from our human goodness, so that he is not good in our sense but in his own—the path of Lucretius among the ancients or of Deism in more recent times. Or (4) we can hold to the belief in an omnipotent, benevolent deity and deny that non-man-caused evil exists. This is the path of most forms of Christianity including Calvinism. Since James wrestled long and hard with this problem we may examine some of these solutions in detail.

The first solution is based on the denial of a supernatural benevolent deity. It argues that if such a being existed, then physical evil could not exist, but physical evil does exist, therefore the supernatural being does not exist. This makes any explanation of physical evil unnecessary; it is simply a fact about the world.

The second solution we will examine below. The third solution denies that the supernatural being is good. At least it distinguishes between two kinds of goodness, divine goodness and human goodness. The supernatural being is good, but it is his own goodness and has nothing to do with us. Our evil is our own and not his. But the question then is: if this being knows we have our own form of pain, and if he ignores it and does nothing about it, is that not in itself evil? Can there really be any sense in which he can be said to be "good" under such a definition?

A more straightforward solution to the problem of evil is the alternative which simply denies that evil exists. It argues that what seems to us to be evil is only an appearance due to our limited understanding. If we knew the whole purpose of the scheme of things, then what appears to us evil would be seen to be really good, so that evil does not really exist—it is an appearance due to ignorance. This sounds satisfactory, but it is difficult to see how it works in such instances as ships foundering in typhoons, whole cities being wiped out by landslides, or the death of young children from uncontrollable diseases or malfunctionings.

A common form of this last solution holds that evil is really good because it is a necessary means to good. It makes moral victory possible, for example. Without evil to be overcome we could not have the sense of moral rectitude that comes from the conquering of evil. This was the solution to the problem that was taken by William James's father. For Henry, Sr., evil was a necessary part of God's plan for a good universe: "We have walked the weary road we have walked, and suffered the bitter things we have suffered, not because God hated or condemned us, or even had the faintest shadow of a quarrel with us, but solely because He loved us with unspeakable love, and wooed us in that unsuspecting way out of the death we have in ourselves. . . ."[7]

Henry, Sr., believed there could be no good without evil, therefore evil was a necessary means to good and this made evil a good. William James was unable to accept this line of argument. If evil was in itself an evil thing and God had to use it as a means to good, then this did not prove that evil was good but rather that God was limited in his power since he was unable to devise a means to good that was itself good.

The problem that haunted William was expressed by his father in this way: "What people in general wish to know, is, not how God may justly condemn evil, but how the opportunity either for condemning or pardoning it arises under his perfect administration."[8]

Two quotations from William James may serve to indicate the direction which he sought to follow in wrestling with this problem. In an entry in his diary for February, 1870, James wrote:

Can one with full knowledge and sincerity ever bring one's self so to sympathize with the total process of the universe as heartily to assent to the evil that seems inherent in its details? . . . though evil slay me, she can't subdue me, or make me worship her. The brute force is all at her command, but the final protest of my soul as she squeezes me out of existence gives me still in a certain sense the superiority.[9]

On another occasion, in a letter to a friend, Mrs. Glendower Evans, James wrote:

Evil is evil and pain is pain; and in bearing them valiantly I think the only thing we can do is to believe that the good power of the world does not appoint them of its own free will, but works under some dark and inscrutable limitations, and that we by our patience and good will, can somehow strengthen his hands.[10]

In these two statements we may find two fundamental themes which illuminate much of James's philosophy. A fundamental doctrine of traditional supernaturalism is the doctrine of the omnipotence of God. This doctrine was developed through St. Augustine and into Calvinism in such detail as to deduce its logically necessary corollary, the doctrine of the impotence of man. If God is everything, if in him resides all power, then it necessarily follows that man is nothing and in him there resides no power whatever. In New England Calvinism this becomes the doctrine that man cannot save himself by any act of his own, he is completely unable to do anything at all to merit his own salvation, he can therefore only be saved by God in whom all power resides. That is, he can only be saved by an act of divine grace, a beneficence conferred upon him by an omnipotent deity. Since God is also omniscient, he had divine foreknowledge of whom he is going to confer this grace upon and whom he is not. From this prescience of God follow all the other substantive doctrines of Calvinism, such as predestination and the doctrine of the elect.

James was unable to accept the doctrine of the impotence of man. From his rejection of this doctrine and his assertion of efficacious powers within man himself follows almost every major tenet of his philosophy that is unique to him. It would perhaps not be an overstatement to say that James cannot argue the efficacy of human endeavor philosophically simply because it is the fundamental tenet of his position. Since all of his philosophy flows from it, he has no philosophy which precedes it, which can justify it. It is, with James, a psychological affirmation, not a philosophical one. It was what he later came to call an act of will as distinguished from an act of reason.

In rejecting the doctrine of the impotence of man James broke the back of New England Calvinism. At the same time he allied himself with the forces in New England and in American thought generally which maintained that the human contribution did count in the scheme of things, that man's fate was not predestined but that his own efforts did, to some extent at least, determine his own life and the course of human events.

In affirming that man could make his own destiny, that he could by his own efforts destroy the barriers which stood between him and the new frontiers—whether these frontiers were geographical or intellectual or social—he reaffirmed man's faith in himself and re-established human dignity. He expressed a doctrine fundamental to the pioneering spirit of those Americans who moved out from New England to explore the continent of North America, and echoed a faith that Calvinism had lost, but that had lived in the Greece of Pericles, that had a rebirth in the Renaissance and enlightenment, and that was essential to any expression of the belief in the dignity of man.

Man is not, in James's view, an impotent being groveling at the feet of an omnipotent deity who casts crumbs of divine grace to undeserving souls here below. For James man has within himself powers which are, at least in part, determinative of not only his own fate but also the fate of the universe. This is a theme which echoes and re-echoes through his writings. Man's efforts must count for something; they must make some difference. If they did not, life would be a farce. This fundamental act of affirming the intrinsic worth and dignity of human life and the significance of human effort is James's response at once to Calvinism and Newtonianism and Darwinism. It is not an affirmation to which James came casually or easily. There was a fundamental ordeal by fire which he went through to reach his own moment of truth. We will examine this crisis more intimately in the discussion below of James's treatment of the problem of free will. But James recognized that this was not a matter of one's philosophy, but of one's psychology, so to speak.

He says:

> . . . when this challenge comes to us, it is simply our total character and personal genius that are on trial; and if we invoke any so-called philosophy, our choice and use of that also are but revelations of our personal aptitude or incapacity for moral life. From this unsparing practical ordeal no professor's lectures and no array of books can save us. The solving word for the learned and the unlearned man alike lies in the last resort in the dumb willingness and unwillingness of their interior characters and nowhere else. It is not in heaven, neither is it beyond the sea; but the word is very nigh unto thee, in thy mouth and in thy heart, that thou mayest do it.[11]

The second of the doctrines developed by James was simply the reverse side of the first. From the omnipotence of God, Calvinism had necessarily deduced the impotence of man. If God was everything, man was nothing. James saw that if we denied the latter of these we must deny the former also. He saw that so far as man had any power to determine the course of events, just so far the determination of events was denied to God. It followed that man's power to effect the fate of himself and his world imposed a necessary limit on God's power to do so. From this James concluded a "finite God," a god upon whose powers there were some limits.

If God had a limited efficacy in determining the course of events so far as they affected human affairs, perhaps he was limited in other areas of action also. Thus James was led to the solution of the problem of evil referred to above in the letter to Mrs. Evans when he said that:

> Evil is evil and pain is pain; and in bearing them valiantly I think the only thing we can do is to believe that the good power of the world does not appoint them of its own free will, but works under some dark and inscrutable limitations, and that we by our patience and good will, can somehow strengthen his hands.

Evil is not, in this view, something God approves of, but he is powerless to prevent it in all cases. He is limited either in power or knowledge or perhaps both. He may know how to eliminate evil but be unable to do it, or he may be able to do it but not know how to go about it. Thus he is either not omnipotent or not omniscient or both. James concludes that we must accept, along with the notion that there is a God, the notion that "he is finite, either in power or in knowledge, or both at once."[12]

Finally, the notion that man has some powers, coupled with the notion that God lacks some powers, enables James to suggest that it may be possible for man's abilities to supplement those of God in such a way that the ultimate fate of things may depend upon man and God working together. James rejects what he calls the optimistic and pessimistic views of the universe—the one asserting that the universe is necessarily getting better, the other that it is necessarily getting worse—for the view he labels "meliorism," which is the view that the universe is not necessarily becoming anything. It is an "open universe"; what it will become is not determined. It may get better or it may get worse. Which outcome prevails may depend upon what man and God working together are able to accomplish. We will examine these notions in some detail in the following chapters.

James thus restores to human life and human effort a significance and a dignity denied it by the notion of an absolute deity. For James, who disliked absolutes in any guise, the notion of an absolute deity, like that of an absolute king, was inconsistent with the notion of the dignity of the individual. The ultimate issue of things resides partly in God's hands and partly in ours. "He helps us and we can help him."[13] In restoring significance to human life, James also restored to it responsibility. Man is responsible for the ultimate issue of things. His efforts do count. Let him, then, use them wisely.

Chapter 2

PSYCHOLOGY: MIND AND BODY

William James wrote his famous two-volume treatise *The Principles of Psychology* in the years from 1878 to 1890. It was the first thoroughgoing description of the new experimental psychology. It was an instant success and—in spite of its nearly 1400 pages—is still available in reprint.

Ralph Barton Perry, a student of William James, has remarked in his Pulitzer Prize biography of James that, at the time James undertook his writing of *The Principles of Psychology*, ". . . the psychological problem which interested him most deeply was that of the relation between mind and body. This problem stood at the crossroads where science met religion and where physiology met psychology."[1] This problem was in fact the other side of the issue that concerned James so intensely and which we have examined in the previous chapter. In considering the relation of science to religion, if one looked out into the world about him he encountered the problem of evil and man's relation to God. If he turned the science-religion matter inward he met the problem of the relation of mind (soul) to body and its ancillary problem, the free-will–determinism issue.

The mind-body problem entered philosophy in the work of the seventeenth-century French philosopher René Descartes. Descartes thought that if he could separate mind and body, then science could proceed without interference from religion. Religion could have the mind (soul) and science the body of man and there would be no jurisdictional disputes.

In developing the dichotomy between mind and body, Descartes separated the two so completely that no efforts since his time have been able to reunite them. The mind-body problem remains as one of the standing problems of contemporary philosophy.

The mind-body problem arises out of a realization of the drastic intrinsic difference between that which is mental and that which is material. To delineate the basic outlines of the problem we may focus first on the fundamental element in each of them. In the case of matter the fundamental entity is an atom; in the case of mind it is an idea. Without being unduly subtle we may say that an atom is a physical object which has mass and occupies space. An idea is a psychic object which is part of the conscious experience of some individual. It does not have mass or occupy a point in space. In the ordinary course of events, we expect atoms and ideas to operate independently of one another. If a chemist is performing an experiment, he does not expect that his ideas about the atoms in his chemical substances will in any way affect the behavior of the atoms. Atoms are affected only by other atoms. The only thing which influences matter is matter.

If I should stand so I have no physical contact with a chair and should then will that the chair should move, no one would expect it to do so. My ideas do not interact causally with physical objects. The way to move a chair is to use another physical object—my hand, for example. This notion of the inviolate integrity of the physical world is a fundamental postulate of all physical science. Nothing need be taken into account by the physical scientist except physical objects and physical forces. These represent the only causally efficacious entities in the world of science.

But if we press the problem one step further we strike a curious anomaly. When I willed that the chair should move, nothing happened. I had to use the physical object "hand" to move it. But now I observe the strange phenomenon that when I willed that the physical object "hand" should move, lo and behold, it did so. We find the startling situation that in the case of many of the physical behaviors of my own body my ideas appear to be causally efficacious. They violate the integrity of the physical realm and introduce psychic constituents into the causal chain.

This flow of energies can also reverse itself. When I engage in the physical act of touching the chair, this physical process will engender psychic experiences, that is, ideas of smoothness, hardness, etc. This intermingling of the causal chain of physical and psychic forces is known philosophically as interactionism.

Descartes was an interactionist. He argued that mind and body were intrinsically different but that they interacted with one another. He located the seat of the interaction in the pineal gland—a newly discovered physiological structure whose function was unknown and which was conveniently located at the base of the brain.

Descartes succeeded in convincing philosophers of the inherent difference between physical and mental phenomena, but the problem of how these could interact could not be solved by saying that the interaction was "located" in the pineal gland. Such a statement does not solve the problem, it only hides it.

The Dutch philosopher Spinoza and the German philosopher Leibniz developed major segments of their philosophies while trying to solve the mind-body problem. They did not notably succeed. In the nineteenth century with the rise of psychology this problem cried for attention. William James as a leading psychologist of the period could not remain aloof from the controversy.

Both Descartes and James were interactionists. That is, they believed that the psychic or mental chain of ideas interacted with the physical or material causal chain of physiological functionings. One might have thought that Descartes' failure to deal successfully with this problem was due to the inadequate state of knowledge of human psychology in his day. However, two hundred years later in William James's day, after some tremendous strides in psychology and physiology, the resolution of the problem seemed even further away. Today, almost a century away from the period when James first wrote on this problem, our greatly increased knowledge of psychology has only served to make a solution to the problem seem even less likely.

The basic issue is how to bridge the gap between the mental and the physical. As psychological knowledge has increased, psychologists have found no need to resort to a concern for "mentalistic" phenomena in order to explain human behavior. The ways we behave seem to be entirely explicable by resort solely to physical forces operative upon us and within us. Are we, then, merely automata, responding in terms of our physical structures to the physical energies which impinge upon our receptor mechanisms? We seem to be conscious of what is going on, but our consciousness does not affect what goes on. We are like spectators living within a mechanically functioning organism and observing what happens to it, without being able to control or affect it. This notion that we are only beings who are conscious of the functioning of the automaton in which we reside was dubbed in James's day the "conscious-automaton" theory.[2] It was the theory James was concerned to deny.

In *The Principles* James quotes a passage from Huxley:

It seems to me that in men, as in brutes, there is no proof that any state of consciousness is the cause of change in the motion of the matter of the organism. If these positions are well based, it follows that our mental conditions are simply the symbols in consciousness of the changes which take place automatically in the organism; and that, to take an extreme illustration, the feeling we call volition is not the cause of a voluntary act, but the symbol of that state of the brain which is the immediate cause of that act.[3]

James also quotes an illuminating passage from Tyndall:

The passage from the physics of the brain to the corresponding facts of consciousness is unthinkable. Granted that a definite thought and a definite molecular action in the brain occur simultaneously; we do not possess the intellectual organs, nor apparently any rudiment of the organ, which would enable us to pass, by a process of reasoning, from one to the other.[4]

When James began his acquaintance with physiology, he was himself an advocate of this theory. In the chapter of *The Principles* titled "The Automaton-Theory," he tells us in a footnote:

The present writer recalls how in 1869, when still a medical student, he began to write an essay showing how almost everyone who speculated about brain-processes illicitly interpolated into his account of them links derived from the entirely heterogenous universe of feeling [consciousness]. . . . The writing was soon stopped because he perceived that the view he was upholding against these authors was a pure conception, with no proofs to be adduced of its reality. Later it seemed to him that whatever *proofs* existed really told in favor of their views.[5]

In fact, in discussing the conscious-automaton theory in *The Principles,* James pointed out that the theory led to a more drastic conclusion than even its ordinary adherents came to, since it actually required us to assert that the psychic chain had no causal efficacy even mentally. The links, so to speak, were not linked. He says:

Another inference, apparently more paradoxical still, needs to be made, though, as far as I am aware, Dr. Hodgson is the only writer who has explicitly drawn it. That inference is that feelings, not causing nerve-actions, cannot even cause each other. To ordinary common sense, felt pain is, as such, not only the cause of outward tears and cries, but also the cause of such inward events as sorrow, compunction, desire, or inventive thought. So the consciousness of good news is the direct producer of the feeling of joy, the awareness of premises that of the belief in conclusions. But according to the automaton-theory, each of the feelings mentioned is only the correlate of some nerve-movement whose cause lay wholly in a previous nerve-movement. The first nerve-movement called up the second; whatever feeling was attached to the second consequently found itself following upon the feeling that was attached to the

first. If, for example, good news was the consciousness correlated with the first movement, then joy
turned out to be the correlate in consciousness of
the second. But all the while the items of the nerve
series were the only ones in causal continuity; the
items of the consciousness series, however inwardly
rational their sequence, were simply juxtaposed.[6]

It is quite easy to miss the significance of this whole
mind-body problem because the points involved are of
such a subtle quality. Another aspect of it that has been
bothersome—since the time, at least, of Epicurus—is the
problem of what an idea is as a psychological entity.
Epicurus says that physically an idea is the movement
of an atom in the brain. A more sophisticated contemporary physiology describes it as an electric wave moving
across the cortex. But whether we call an idea the movement of an atom or of an electric force the point is that
neither of these is an idea. They may accompany the idea.
But the idea is something quite different; it is mental,
not physical. A moving atom or a moving wave are inanimate physical objects. An idea is not inanimate but
animate, i.e., conscious—in some sense even self-conscious.

Although we may correlate a change in electric poten-
tial from one part of the brain to another part with an
idea, it is not the same thing as an idea—any more than
a change in the acidity state of the mouth when I take
a bite of candy is the idea of sweetness.

All of the various aspects of the mind-body problem—
the causal efficacy of ideas, the relation of ideas to one
another, the nature of idea or mind as psychic entities—
were problems which intrigued James greatly. In seeking
to solve them he developed his own approach, which led
him to his famous notion of the "stream of conscious-

ness" and to the significant analysis of mind as a function rather than a thing. We will examine each of these.

James discusses the nature of mind in Chapter VI of *The Principles of Psychology*. This chapter follows the chapter on the conscious-automaton theory and begins with the admonition that:

> The reader who found himself swamped with too much metaphysics in the last chapter will have a still worse time of it in this one. . . . The fundamental conceptions of psychology are practically very clear to us, but theoretically they are very confused, and one easily makes the obscurest assumptions in this science without realizing, until challenged, what internal difficulties they involve.[7]

I fear I must echo James's concern. The root meaning of *psyche* is soul, so that psychology meant originally the study of the soul. Some wag has said that psychology first lost its soul, then its mind, and now is in danger of losing consciousness altogether. It is to be hoped that the reader will not follow that same path in the ensuing discussion.

James brings a number of points to bear on this problem. He suggests in the first place that ever since David Hume's famous analysis of the causal process in the physical order of things, all that causation has meant scientifically is a constant conjunction or correlation of events. But if we take this to be a definition of cause-effect, then there are appropriate correlations between physical and mental phenomena which require us to say that they are causally connected.

A second point is that consciousness as a causally efficacious instrument is supported by evolutionary arguments. As organisms become increasingly complex the possible modes of response to the environment increase many fold. There should develop, as a survival process, a function of selection among the many possible modes of response. James says: "consciousness is at all times primarily a selecting agency."[8] Consciousness chooses purposes toward which organisms direct their energies, and it selects means appropriate to these purposes. Purposes are left out of mechanical behavior. It is only consciousness which is goal-oriented:

> Real ends appear for the first time now upon the world's stage. . . . Every actually existing consciousness seems to itself at any rate to be a *fighter for ends* of which many, but for its presence, would not be ends at all. Its powers of cognition are mainly subservient to these ends, discerning which facts further them and which do not.[9]

From this selective process the human organism develops awareness of "right" and "wrong." A machine does not have such an awareness, nor is its action guided by it. Even the most physiological biologists argue that animals learn to perform those acts which give them pleasure and to avoid those which give them pain. But this is to assert that the experiences of pleasure and pain are causally efficacious.

All of these arguments lead James to the notion that if there is no direct evidence for interactionism, there is sufficient circumstantial evidence to warrant accepting it. He, accordingly, writes his psychology from that point of view.

We may ask ourselves what kind of thing consciousness is. Or, to put the question more precisely, what is life? How did it get here? The general view, common among biochemists today, is a revised form of the spontaneous-generation theory. It distinguishes between what are sometimes called the resultant properties of matter and the emergent properties. If we combine atoms chemically, the chemical combination, say a molecule, often has properties its constituents did not have. For example, it will have a different physical shape, a greater mass than any of its parts, etc. These properties, however, are the result of similar properties found in the individual atoms. Thus the atomic mass of a water molecule is 18. This results from the fact that it is made of two hydrogen atoms—each of which has an atomic weight of one—and an oxygen atom of weight 16. The resultant mass of 18 in the molecule, then, is a simple additive property from similar properties in its parts.

When we consider some other properties of water molecules, however, we do not find that this additive relation holds. Thus water molecules have the property of "wetness," i.e., water will wet things, although the parts —hydrogen and oxygen—are gases and do not have this property. This new property then is not simply the sum of certain similar properties in the parts, but is a property which has emerged from the combination without being found in the parts. Such properties are called emergent properties.

The contemporary biochemical hypothesis is that "life" or "consciousness" is an emergent property of a certain complex combination of chemical materials.

James knew this theory in its nineteenth-century form, but did not approve of it. He says:

> Let it not be objected that H and O combine themselves into "water," and thenceforward exhibit new properties. They do not. The "water" is just the old atoms in the new position, H-O-H; the "new properties" are just their combined *effects,* when in

this position, upon external media, such as our sense-organs and the various reagents on which water may exert its properties and be known.[10]

A further alternative which James rejects is what he calls "The Mind-Stuff Theory."[11] This is the theory that mind is made up of some kind of immaterial atoms somewhat as matter is made up of material atoms. This "mind-dust" theory is elaborately refuted[12] although it has a merit which the emergent-property theory lacks, namely continuity. James objects to the abrupt introduction of consciousness into the evolutionary process. "If evolution is to work smoothly, consciousness in some shape must have been present at the very origin of things."[13] But in what shape? In a thoroughly Jamesian expression—which tells much about our author—he expostulates:

What shall we do? Many would find relief at this point in celebrating the mystery of the unknowable and the "awe" which we should feel at having such a principle to take final charge of our perplexities. Others would rejoice that the finitist and separatist view of things with which we started had at last developed its contradictions, and was about to lead us dialectically upwards to some "higher synthesis" in which inconsistencies cease from troubling and logic is at rest. It may be a constitutional infirmity, but I can take no comfort in such devices for making a luxury of intellectual defeat. They are but spiritual chloroform. Better live on the ragged edge, better gnaw the file forever![14]

It takes many pages for him to do it, but James eventually comes around to what looks suspiciously like a form of the emergent-property view and which does not provide the continuity from the beginning of things which he felt evolution demanded.

Admitting to an inability to resolve the mind–body interaction—"a stream of thought accompanying a stream of cerebral activity, by a law yet unexplained"[15]—he examines the question of what thinking or conscious thought is. Is it a series of mental phenomena inhering in a mind-stuff or a soul-substance? To assert this is simply to hide the issue in a mystery—to say it over again under another name which explains nothing and hides everything. If we avoid this approach, the only conclusion to which we can come is that thinking is a process, not a thing. There is no mind-substance, there is only a brain-process. Just as breathing is a function of the lungs and walking of the legs—and there is no immaterial substance to which they belong—so thinking is simply the biological functioning of the brain. When "we take the two formulations, first of a brain to whose processes pulses of thought *simply* correspond, and second of one to whose processes pulses of thought *in a soul* correspond, and compare them together, we see that at bottom the second formulation is only a more roundabout way than the first, of expressing the same bald fact. That bald fact is that *when the brain acts, a thought occurs.*"[16]

> Altogether, the Soul is an outbirth of that sort of philosophizing whose great maxim, according to Dr. Hodgson, is: "Whatever you are *totally* ignorant of, assert to be the explanation of everything else."[17]

Having got rid of the mind and the soul, we now have left only a functioning brain producing a stream of thoughts—what James called "the stream of consciousness"—from which selections are made. The process of selection is all we mean by mind, and the ability to select is thinking, or intelligence.

Thus although James did not solve the mind-body problem, he did attain a first modern formulation of it. Mind as an entity disappears. It becomes simply a brain function. The problem of how an inanimate brain produces a conscious, animate thought is left for the future. A relation between the two is asserted on indirect evidence. The notion prevalent since Hume, and fundamental to eighteenth- and nineteenth-century associationist psychology, that consciousness is a series of isolated ideas associated by mental bonds, the atomizing of experience into bundles of isolable sensations, is denied. Substituted for this atomistic consciousness is a continuum of consciousness—a stream of consciousness. Where for Hume, and the associationists, the problem was how to unite the isolated experiences given in sensation, James unites them as given, so that for him the problem is how to divide consciousness up into segments which are biologically useful and aesthetically and morally significant.

From this general analysis of consciousness as a stream of thought out of which each individual carves his own personal identity was to grow James's pragmatism as the theory that concepts are formed by selecting out of this continuum in terms of individual purposes. His neutral monism in metaphysics is to be traced to it also as we shall see in a later chapter.

As a direct result of this new psychology there was to grow up in American literature a "stream of consciousness" school of writing. Probably no historian of literature could write a more succinct account of the philosophy of this school than that statement which James made at the close of his chapter on "The Stream of Thought," in which he heralded its birth.

Looking back, then, over this review, we see that the mind is at every stage a theatre of simultaneous possibilities. Consciousness consists in the comparison of these with each other, the selection of some, and the suppression of the rest by the reinforcing and inhibiting agency of attention. The highest and most elaborated mental products are filtered from the data chosen by the faculty next beneath, out of the mass offered by the faculty below that, which mass in turn was sifted from a still larger amount of yet simpler material, and so on. The mind, in short, works on the data it receives very much as a sculptor works on his block of stone. In a sense the statue stood there from eternity. But there were a thousand different ones beside it, and the sculptor alone is to thank for having extricated this one from the rest. Just so the world of each of us, howsoever different our several views of it may be, all lay embedded in the primordial chaos of sensations, which gave the mere *matter* to the thought of all of us indifferently. We may, if we like, by our reasonings unwind things back to that black and jointless continuity of space and moving clouds of swarming atoms which science calls the only real world. But all the while the world *we* feel and live in will be that which our ancestors and we, by slowly cumulative strokes of choice, have extricated out of this, like sculptors, by simply rejecting certain portions of the given stuff. Other sculptors, other statues from the same stone! Other minds, other worlds from the same monotonous and inexpressive chaos! My world is but one in a million alike embedded, alike real to those who may abstract them. How different must be the worlds in the consciousness of ant, cuttle-fish, or crab![18]

The other concept involved in the conscious-automaton theory was the notion of the automaton: Is human behavior completely determined by a combination of environmental forces and inherited structures, or are human beings free to act in ways not controlled by such forces? This is an important philosophical question primarily because of its impact on the problems of ethics. There is no point in telling a man he ought to do things if he cannot do them. Nor is there any point in telling him he ought to do them if he can only do something else. The fundamental ethical action is the action of choosing between alternatives. It is fruitless to assert that a man ought to do action A if he can only do action B. Nor is there any sense in telling him to do B if he can only do B. Without freedom of choice between alternatives, ethical statements—"ought" statements—are meaningless.

The ethical philosopher seeks to establish values; in terms of these values he prescribes "norms" or normal patterns of behavior. Individuals "ought" to act in accord with these norms. The ethical philosopher does not believe himself to be simply describing how people do in fact act; description is the function of science. The ethical philosopher is "prescribing" how people ought to act— which is quite often different from the description of how they do act. Hence science is a descriptive process and ethics is a prescriptive, or normative, process.

But to prescribe norms in terms of which people ought to act is a waste of time unless they can act this way. Accordingly, without free will, ethics is meaningless. On the other hand, if a scientist of human behavior—a psychologist—attains to a description of how human beings do in fact behave and then some human being exercises his free will to act in some other way, he invalidates the description and ruins the science. Thus ethics is impossible *without* free will, and psychology as a science of causal order is impossible *with* it. This poses a nice problem for a philosopher-psychologist like William James if he wishes to develop an ethical philosophy that is compatible with his psychology.

Before William James's *Psychology* appeared, the study of psychology required that it be a normative science; James, following Darwin's cue in biology, undertook to make psychology a descriptive science. Some commentators see this as James's most significant contribution to psychology.

But if we make psychology a descriptive science we introduce the problem that has haunted psychology ever since James: what shall we do with normative behavior?

The problem came to the fore largely as a result of Darwin's work. Darwin proposed, in effect, a continuum between man and the natural world which had been denied before his time. Prior to Darwin the limits of science had been thought of as stopping short of living beings. Science, as it developed out of Newton and classical physics, was the establishing of unwavering laws describing cause-effect relations. Living organisms, and particularly human beings, were thought to be exempt from absolute laws so far as their organic nature was concerned. Thus the scheme of things could be divided into the realm of science and the realm of organic behavior. In the former there was determinism. In the latter there was room for a certain indeterminism, a certain violation of cause-effect relationships. One of the most dramatic by-products of Darwinism was to contradict this notion of a divided universe. Darwin's analysis of the origination of new species by the process of sporting and natural selection argued that the scientific methodology previously thought to be applicable only to physics and chemistry was applicable to the life processes as well.

This raised some difficulties. If the same methodology

could be used to explain the phenomena found in both the realm of the physical sciences and the realm of the life processes, this suggested a continuum. It suggested no sharp division between these two areas but rather that the life processes were part of science just as much as the physical processes were. And so we attained the life "sciences" and the physical sciences. Both of them, being sciences, were thought to be subject to law. From this concept of law as applicable to organic behavior was to develop zoology, botany, psychology, and sociology. These sciences, like all sciences, depend upon the formulation of cause-effect relations which make explanation and prediction possible. Thus a psychiatrist who has a patient who is paranoid does not shrug his shoulders and say the patient willed to become paranoiac. He searches for the cause of the condition, believing that it has a cause which if found and eliminated will alleviate the condition. Similarly a sociologist presented with an increase of juvenile delinquency in a community does not pass it off by attributing it to the free will of the delinquents. He assumes a cause, the removal of which will lead to a decrease in the incidence of delinquency.

So far, then, as the life sciences—biology, psychology, sociology—are sciences of life processes, they assume causal laws determinative of the effects observed. This is what is meant by determinism in science: every event is completely controlled by its causes,* so that if we knew all the causes we could predict the event entirely.

Those who subscribe to the doctrine of free will wish to deny that determinism is applicable to all of human behavior. They contend that the human will violates the mechanical cause-effect chain so that the human being's

---

* In more recent twentieth-century science this would become "statistically controlled."

actions are not completely determined by his circumstances.

William James does not feel that he can "prove" that free will exists. But he thinks we can assume it to be true. Our first act of freedom, if we are free, he says, ought to be to freely affirm our freedom. But if we grant that free will cannot be proved, why should we assume it? James's essay "The Dilemma of Determinism" is written to show why free will should be assumed.[19]

In his prefatory remarks to this essay James states explicitly two premises which condition his thinking not only about this matter but about religion generally. They represent fundamental presuppositions of James's whole philosophical effort. He says:

The arguments I am about to urge all proceed on two suppositions: first, when we make theories about the world and discuss them with one another, we do so in order to attain a conception of things which shall give us subjective satisfaction; and, second, if there be two conceptions, and the one seems to us, on the whole, more rational than the other, we are entitled to suppose that the more rational one is the truer of the two. I hope that you are willing to make these suppositions with me; for I am afraid that if there be any of you here who are not, they will find little edification in the rest of what I have to say. I cannot stop to argue the point; but I myself believe that all the magnificent achievements of mathematical and physical science—our doctrines of evolution, of uniformity of law, and the rest—proceed from our indomitable desire to cast the world into a more rational shape in our minds than the shape into which it is thrown there by the crude order of our experience. The world has shown itself, to a great extent, plastic to this demand of ours for rationality. How much further it will show itself plastic no one can say. Our only means of finding out is to try; and I, for one, feel as free to try conceptions of moral as of mechanical or of logical rationality. If a certain formula for expressing the nature of the world violates my moral demand, I shall feel as free to throw it overboard, or at least to doubt it, as if it disappointed my demand for uniformity of sequence, for example; the one demand being, so far as I can see, quite as subjective and emotional as the other is. The principle of causality, for example,—what is it but a postulate, an empty name covering simply a demand that the sequence of events shall some day manifest a deeper kind of belonging of one thing with another than the mere arbitrary juxtaposition which now phenomenally appears? It is as much an altar to an unknown god as the one that Saint Paul found at Athens. All our scientific and philosophic ideals are altars to unknown gods. Uniformity is as much so as is free-will. If this be admitted, we can debate on even terms. But if any one pretends that while freedom and variety are, in the first instance, subjective demands, necessity and uniformity are something altogether different, I do not see how we can debate at all.[20]

The introduction by James of a subjective feeling (in nineteenth-century terminology a "sentiment") as the ultimate criterion in philosophy is the most serious difficulty in his whole system. His critics have complained over and over about him in this respect. It is not so difficult to point out the weaknesses of this position. It is more difficult to analyze its strengths.

In what may well be the most basic statement James ever made of his philosophical *Weltanschauung,* the essay titled "The Sentiment of Rationality," James raises what may be the most fundamental of philosophical inquiries:

What is the task which philosophers set themselves to perform; and why do they philosophize at all? Almost every one will immediately reply: They desire to attain a conception of the frame of things which shall on the whole be more rational than that somewhat chaotic view which every one by nature carries about with him under his hat. But suppose this rational conception attained, how is the philosopher to recognize it for what it is, and not let it slip through ignorance? The only answer can be that he will recognize its rationality as he recognizes everything else, by certain subjective marks with which it affects him. When he gets the marks, he may know that he has got the rationality.

What, then, are the marks? A strong feeling of ease, peace, rest, is one of them. The transition from a state of puzzle and perplexity to rational comprehension is full of lively relief and pleasure.

. . . This feeling of the sufficiency of the present moment, of its absoluteness,—this absence of all need to explain it, account for it, or justify it,—is what I call the Sentiment of Rationality. As soon, in short, as we are enabled from any cause whatever to think with perfect fluency, the thing we think of seems to us *pro tanto* rational.*[21]

This paradoxical notion that rationality is a sentiment will be repugnant to many persons. Rationality is reason

---

* This statement should be compared with the notion of doubt and belief in Charles Peirce's essay on "The Fixation of Belief."

and sentiment is emotion and there is no connection between the two! But how do we distinguish between two
different chains of argument when we say one is reasonable and the other is unreasonable? Well, the answer
might be: one is logical and the other is not. But James's
question is more fundamental. Given two sets of premises
leading to two different conclusions, we will say that one
set, say set A, is logical and the other set, set B, is not.
Now, in making this decision we had some standard,
"X," we call "being logical" in mind. We took this
standard "X" and measured set A against it and found
that set A conformed to the standard; we took the standard and measured set B against it and found that set
B did not conform. James's question is: where did we
get the standard "X"? When we come to decide what
the standard of "being logical" is there will be a number
of alternatives which will present themselves—X, Y, Z,
U, V, W, etc. How do we decide among these alternatives? We cannot pick the one which is most logical—
because we do not yet have a standard of logic; that is
what we are trying to determine. Before we have a standard of logic, then, how do we decide, among alternative
"logics" presented for our selection, the one we all accept as "most" logical? There must be some criterion of a
nonlogical character which we use since we have not yet
got any logical criterion because we have no logic. The
criterion of selection, says James, must be emotive in
nature, that is, subjective. We will select the one which
leads us to a "feeling of ease, peace, rest," which provides a "transition from a state of puzzle and perplexity
to . . . lively relief and pleasure."

The same doctrine is expressed by James nearly twenty years later as the fundamental thesis of the essay "The
Will to Believe":

Our passional nature not only lawfully may, but must, decide an option between propositions, whenever it is a genuine option that cannot be decided on intellectual grounds; for to say, under such circumstances, "Do not decide, but leave the question open," is itself a passional decision,—just like deciding yes or no,—and is attended with the same risk of losing the truth.[22]

If we proceed on this presupposition and examine the free-will issue, we find that there are no conclusive intellectual arguments on either side. Given a particular action, when you ask a determinist to explain its causes he will often admit that he cannot; if you wish to conclude from this that determinism is false, he will not allow this inference to be drawn. He will say that there were causes for the action, but the science of human behavior is not yet advanced far enough to be able to say what they were. If an advocate of free will replies that the reason we cannot find the causes of the action is because it had no binding causes but rather was freely willed, the determinist will rightly reply: you can't prove that either.

So we find we cannot prove that determinism is true, or that it is false; we cannot prove that free will is true or that it is false. What do we do under such circumstances? Well, says James, we can let our emotive nature choose. We can pick the view we would like to have true, the view that seems most fitting, the view that gives us a universe in which we have a "feeling of ease, peace, rest"; a universe which would take us from "a state of puzzle and perplexity to . . . lively relief and pleasure." Which universe would this be? The universe of the free-willist or that of the determinist? The answer to this question could be a matter of taste. And James admits this.

But his point is that since these two options are both available to us for acceptance—that is, neither one can be proved false—and since we should select the one that is in accord with our sentiment of rationality, then no error of logic or fact can be charged against the man who selects the free-will option if this is in accord with his feeling about what would be most rational.

In an effort to decide which universe would be most rational, James (in the macabre fashion of the nineteenth-century horror story) asks us to consider "the confession of the murderer at Brockton the other day: how, to get rid of the wife whose continued existence bored him, he inveigled her into a desert spot, shot her four times, and then, as she lay on the ground and said to him, 'You didn't do it on purpose, did you dear?' replied, 'No, I didn't do it on purpose,' as he raised a rock and smashed her skull."

James says that for himself he finds such an action to be a bad moral fit with his notion of how the universe ought to be run. As a free-willist he can blame it on the free choice of the murderer. But the determinist for whom the action is fully determined from all eternity must blame it on the creator of the universe, and if the actions of the creator produce the best possible scheme of things, then this action must be a good action. No better action could have taken its place or a good creator would have provided for its doing so. Therefore this must be the best of all possible actions and therefore the most rational of all possible actions. James refuses to accept this. He knows there are other possible actions and he refuses to say some of them would not have been better. "There are *some* instinctive reactions which I, for one, will not tamper with."[23]

Following his principle of choosing between equally plausible alternatives that one which gives rise to a sentiment of rationality, a feeling of ease, peace, and rest, James elects the free-will alternative as being the only one which allows for such a possibility, as the Brockton murder, without requiring us to say that it is good.

From this affirmation of human free will, James moved easily into a discussion of ethics. If man can act freely, what must he do to provide a world in which there is more good and less evil? Proceeding on the principle that the function of philosophy is to find a rational scheme of things, James begins his exercise in moral philosophy by saying that moral philosophy cannot end in skepticism.[24] To become a skeptic is to deny that a system of morals is possible. But this choice results not from having developed a moral philosophy but rather from having given up philosophy. The job of philosophy, says James, is to unify and systematize. Skepticism claims such unifying to be impossible. Skepticism, then, rather than being one possible issue of moral philosophy, really results from having given up all philosophy.

The problem of the philosopher of morals is not whether a system of morality is possible, but rather what is the best (i.e., most rational) system possible? In this context, again, "most rational" means that view among the available alternatives that gives us a "feeling of ease, peace, rest." Again, there will be many persons who will wish to part company with James here. The most common charge against James, and in fact against his fellow pragmatists Charles S. Peirce and John Dewey as well, is that their whole philosophy is too subjective. Is there no point of objectivity upon which things can rest? We have seen James fall into repeated difficulties on this point. In his discussion of religion he could not settle the religious question by resort to an objective authority. The problem of how to select between the alternatives "God" or "no-god," each claiming equal "objectiveness," forced us to see that the decision of objectivity in religion resolved itself into a decision of which of the "objective alternatives" we found subjectively most satisfying. Again, in logic, the problem of how to select among alternative logics, each claiming to be equally "logical," forced us to see that the decision of which of the alternative logics was most "objective" resolved itself into a decision of which of the "objective alternatives" we found subjectively most satisfying. Finally, in ethics, the problem of how to select among alternative systems of morality the one which is best resolves itself into a decision of which of the alternatives we find subjectively most satisfying.

What James appears, in some significant way, to be saying is that the decision as to what "system of things" we accept as objective is itself not resolvable by objective criteria but only by subjective criteria.

To many persons it would seem as though the whole history of science has run against this belief. Science, we are told, has no room for subjective feelings; science settles its problems by objective means. It resorts to "facts," which are not theories produced by some armchair philosopher. Science gave all that up when it gave up being "natural philosophy."

Since this is one of the most fundamental points in James's whole philosophy, and since it is the point at which his critics have made their sharpest attack, it would be well to digress long enough to take a close look at it.

James has forced himself to the most tantalizing question in the philosophy of modern science: "What exactly, is a scientific 'theory,' and how do we decide among alternative theories presented for our belief?"

When James asks: "How do we decide among alternative theories of religion or of logic or of morals?" many of his critics reply that these theories should be treated as scientific theories and decided as we decide among alternative scientific theories, i.e., by resort to objective fact.

The notion that "objectivity" of the sort here suggested is possible in science has come to be questioned increasingly in recent years. In 1928 the British physicist and astronomer Sir Arthur Eddington began his Gifford Lectures with this statement:

> I have settled down to the task of writing these lectures and have drawn up chairs to my two tables. . . . One of them has been familiar to me from earliest years. It is a commonplace object of that environment which I call the world. How shall I describe it? It has extension; it is comparatively permanent; it is coloured; above all it is substantial. . . . After all if you are a plain commonsense man, not too much worried with scientific scruples, you will be confident that you understand the nature of an ordinary table. . . .
>
> Table No. 2 is my scientific table. It is a more recent acquaintance and I do not feel so familiar with it. It does not belong to the world previously mentioned—the world which spontaneously appears around me when I open my eyes. . . . My scientific table is mostly emptiness. Sparsely scattered in that emptiness are numerous electric charges rushing about with great speed; but their combined bulk amounts to less than a billionth of the bulk of the table itself. . . .
>
> I need not tell you that modern physics has by delicate test and remorseless logic assured me that my second scientific table is the only one which is really there. . . . On the other hand I need not tell you that modern physics will never succeed in exorcising that first table . . . which lies visible to my

eyes and tangible to my grasp. We must bid good-
bye to it for the present for we are about to turn
from the familiar world to the scientific world re-
vealed by physics. This is, or is intended to be, a
wholly external world.[25]

The world of science may be an external world, but
as Eddington's illustration makes clear, it is a world we
never see. It is a world made up to "explain" the behavior of the world we do see. It is a theory about things
we experience. But how do we decide between theories
if we are a scientist? We find, if we pursue any scientific
phenomena far enough, that there are certain fundamental theories which account equally well for the phenomena
observed. The problem of how to decide among alternative theories is a crucial one for science.

A pivotal point in the history of science was the decision to accept the Copernican theory rather than the
Ptolemaic theory of the solar system. On what basis was
the decision between the two made? Each theory accounted for all the observed facts. It is customary to appeal at this point to the so-called law of parsimony, or
Occam's razor, which admonishes a scientist to always
accept the "simpler" theory. But it is not so easy to know
what we mean by simpler. Do we mean, for example,
mathematically simple—can be expressed in a single formula like $E=Mc^2$—or conceptually simple—can be easily
grasped even by a novice—or what? James would say
that, all other things being equal, we should accept, between theories, the one which gives us the greater satisfaction. To this many modern philosophers of science
would agree.

A physical chemist, Michael Polanyi, in a recent book
with the suggestive title *Personal Knowledge,* has this to
say:

What is the true lesson of the Copernican revolution? Why did Copernicus exchange his actual terrestrial station for an imaginary solar standpoint? The only justification for this lay in the greater intellectual satisfaction he derived from the celestial panorama as seen from the sun instead of the earth. Copernicus gave preference to man's delight in abstract theory, at the price of rejecting the evidence of our senses, which present us with the irresistible fact of the sun, the moon, and the stars rising daily in the east to travel across the sky towards their setting in the west. In a literal sense, therefore, the new Copernican system was as anthropocentric as the Ptolemaic view, the difference being merely that it preferred to satisfy a different human affection. . . . It becomes legitimate to regard the Copernican system as more objective than the Ptolemaic only if we accept this very shift in the nature of intellectual satisfaction as the criterion of greater objectivity.[26]

The philosopher Milton K. Munitz, in a recent book titled *Space, Time and Creation,* reached this conclusion:

At best there are as many ways of expressing what the facts are in theoretic terms as man's ingenuity allows him to devise. . . . It makes no sense to say that there is an absolutely best one. Theories are apt or fitting but they are not as such true. . . .[27]

A similar point of view has been maintained by the physicist P. W. Bridgman, who says:

We are thus faced with a radically new situation which may well alter the entire future of theory building. Doubtless a great many alternative theories will be possible, and we shall have to choose between them on grounds of simplicity or convenience of calculation or perhaps on purely aesthetic considerations.[28]

It would appear that if James resolves his fundamental dilemmas by choosing, between equally plausible theories, the one which gives him the greatest subjective satisfaction, he is in fact only adopting the technique used by the "objective" scientist.

Does this mean that all theories are equally good as we find that satisfaction follows from adopting one or the other of them? Clearly not, although many critics insist on reading James in this way. James is talking about theories which account equally well for the observed facts and which have equal predictive power—God or no-god, mind-stuff or brain-process, determinism or free will; given theories like these where we cannot see any differences between them on other grounds, we are then entitled to make a decision on subjective grounds—to accept the theory we would prefer to have true and to act as though it were true. If nothing else, by acting upon it we put it to the test.

We return, then, to an examination of alternative moral theories, looking for a theory which will account for all the facts, have predictive power, and give us a feeling of subjective satisfaction.

Again, we find that there are alternative theories—that morality has a divine origin or that it has a human origin—which are equally plausible.

A theory is designed to unify a set of facts. If the facts are physical facts, then the theory is a physical theory. If the facts are moral facts, then the theory is an ethical theory. What are the facts which a theory of ethics must unify?

James begins his analysis with a discussion of what he calls the psychological question:[29] What is the origin of our moral ideas and judgments? Where do they come from? He says there are, generally, two positions on this point: that of the intuitionist and that of the evolutionist. The intuitionist thinks we have a moral faculty, the conscience—which is generally considered to have a divine origin—which enables us to know, intuitively and independently of experience, what things are good and what things bad. The evolutionist, on the other hand, proposes to explain all of our notions of good and bad by resort to the experiences of the race. Those traits which have had a survival value have come to be called good. Those which have operated against survival have come to be considered bad.

James rejects both of these as being unsatisfactory accounts. His own position is, however, a mixture of elements from both. He labels it "the back-door theory."[30] This theory admits that the intuitionists are right in holding that "The mind has a native structure,"[31] which is to say that certain ways of thinking are natural to it. Thus the laws of logic: "A is A"; the laws of arithmetic: "$2+2=4$," are such that "no other way of considering and no other results are possible . . ."[32] "There is thus a large body of *a priori* or intuitively necessary truths."[33] These a priori ways in which we must think of the world if we are to think of it at all are "due neither to our own nor to our ancestors' experiences."[34] "Our consciousness of these relations no doubt has a natural genesis. But it is to be sought rather in the inner forces which have made the brain grow, than in any mere paths of 'frequent' association which outer stimuli may have ploughed into that organ."[35] That is, as the human brain grew, it grew in certain ways. Its growth and development as a problem-solving tool were necessary for human survival. But it did not have to grow into the particular mode of problem-solving which it did. It could have grown into some other. But having developed as it did, it gives us, by its structure, certain "natural" modes of thinking about the world. The effort of science is to so order our experiences with the empirical world that they fit into these modes of thinking. ". . . the mechanical philosophy [classical physics] is only a way of conceiving nature so as to arrange its items along some of the more natural lines of cleavage of our mental structure."[36]

These logical and mathematical ways of thinking are not the only natural ones, however. "Other natural lines are the moral and aesthetic relations. Philosophy is still seeking to conceive things so that these relations also may seem to obtain between them. . . . So far it has proved easier to identify nature's things with mental terms of the mechanical than with mental terms of the sentimental order."[37]

There are certain natural ways of thinking the world. Some of these are logical and mathematical. The job of science is to so schematize the natural order of things that the world of experience can be thought scientifically in these natural ways. Some of these natural ways are moral and aesthetic. The job of philosophy is to so schematize the natural world that it can be thought morally and aesthetically in these natural ways.

This structure of the mind is "due neither to our own nor to our ancestors' experience." James develops here a Darwinian analysis of mental growth as a function of brain evolution. The brain tissue he conceives of as a highly unstable material in which changes readily occur with slight cause—accidentally and incidentally. Those changes which have survival value are preserved, the others disappear. As concomitants of these changes there are "side-effects" or "back-door" effects, not directly caused by our experiences and with no survival value, which appear fortuitously as related to these changes. These effects are inborn inasmuch as they are brain functions, not experience-conditioned responses. But they are not deliberately produced by the action of survival forces; they are incidental results accompanying changes which are themselves caused by survival forces. Among these many incidental results are moral and aesthetic sensibilities.

In talking about the causes of mental modification, James says:

Some of them are molecular accidents [i.e., genetic mutations] before birth; some of them are collateral and remote combinations, unintended combinations, one might say, of more direct effects wrought in the unstable and intricate brain-tissue. Such a result is unquestionably the susceptibility to music, which some individuals possess at the present day. It has no zoological utility; it corresponds to no object in the natural environment; it is a pure *incident* of having a hearing organ, an incident depending on such instable and inessential conditions that one brother may have it and another brother not. Just so with the susceptibility to sea-sickness, which, so far from being engendered by long experience of its "object" (if a heaving deck can be called its object) is erelong annulled thereby. Our higher aesthetic, moral, and intellectual life seems made up of affections of this collateral and incidental sort, which have entered the mind by the back stairs, as it were, or rather have not entered the mind at all, but got surreptitiously born in the house. No one can successfully treat of phychogenesis, or the factors of mental evolution, without distinguishing between these two ways in which the mind is assailed.[38]

A little later in the same chapter James discusses the aesthetic and moral principles which are thus innate. He says that "The aesthetic principles are that a note sounds good with its third and fifth, or that potatoes need salt."[39] The reader is invited to ask himself why it is that a note sounds good with its third and fifth. This "fact" is not the result of learned experience, since we have a pleasing aesthetic response the first time we hear this combination. If we grant that it is an inborn trait, it is equally difficult to see how it can be attributed to experiences of our ancestors, i.e., how it can be said to be due to survival experiences. What possible survival value can this fact have had that would have led to its preservation as a characteristic of the human auditory apparatus?

James concludes:

We are once for all so made that when certain impressions come before our mind, one of them will seem to call for or repel the others as its companions. To a certain extent the principle of habit will explain these aesthetic connections. When a conjunction is repeatedly experienced the cohesion of its terms grows grateful, or at least their disruption grows unpleasant. But to explain *all* aesthetic judgments in this way would be absurd; for it is notorious how seldom natural experiences come up to our aesthetic demands. . . .

The *moral* principles which our mental structure engenders are quite as little explicable *in toto* by habitual experiences having bred inner cohesions. Rightness is not *mere* usualness, wrongness not *mere*

oddity, however numerous the facts which might
be invoked to prove such identity. Nor are the moral
judgments those most invariably and emphatically
impressed on us by public opinion. The most charac-
teristically and peculiarly moral judgments that a
man is ever called on to make are in unprecedented
cases and lonely emergencies, where no popular rhe-
torical maxims can avail, and the hidden oracle alone
can speak; and it speaks often in favor of conduct
quite unusual, and suicidal as far as gaining popular
approbation goes. The forces which conspire to this
resultant are subtle harmonies and discords between
the elementary ideas which form the data of the case.
Some of these harmonies, no doubt, have to do with
habit; but in respect to most of them our sensibility
must assuredly be a phenomenon of supernumerary
order correlated with a brain-function quite as secondary as that which takes cognizance of the diverse
excellence of elaborate musical compositions. No
more than the higher musical sensibility can the
higher moral sensibility be accounted for by the frequency with which outer relations have cohered.
Take judgments of justice or equity, for example.
Instinctively, one judges everything differently, according as it pertains to one's self or to someone
else. Empirically one notices that everybody else
does the same. But little by little there dawns in one
the judgment "nothing can be right for me which
would not be right for another similarly placed"; or
"the fulfillment of my desires is intrinsically no more
imperative than that of anyone else's"; or "what
it is reasonable that another should do for me, it is
also reasonable that I should do for him"; and forth-
with the whole mass of the habitual gets overturned.

It gets *seriously* overturned only in a few fanatical heads. But its overturning is due to a back-door and not to a front-door process.[40]

These latter generalized ethical principles are called by James "postulates of rationality." Other such postulates that are mentioned by him are "the individual and universal good are one" and "happiness and goodness are bound to coalesce in the same subject."[41]

These postulates of rationality in ethics are analogous to postulates of rationality in science. In the latter case we have such postulates as "Nature is simple and invariable," *"Ex nihilo nihil fit,"* "A thing can only work where it is," etc.[42] These are postulates because science does not try to prove them. They are rational in our earlier sense of providing a subjective sense of ease and peace. Science does not get them from experience—they are "natural cleavages of the mind"—but rather, using them, it seeks to order experience in conformity to what seems to the mind to be rational. So also with the moral postulates. We do not get them from experience, but rather, using them, we seek for an ordering of experience that will conform to these as norms. So far as we fail, they remain empty postulates. So far as we succeed, moral experience is resolved from chaos into a rational order.

Experience resists translation into a rational scheme, whether we are doing science or morals. The task of conceptualizing experience so that it conforms to these postulates—and of reinterpreting the postulates to make the conceptualizing possible—is a continuous one. While progress is being made, it is made slowly and there is no end in sight in either science or morals. Thus James tells us: "there can be no final truth in ethics any more than in physics, until the last man has had his experience and said his say."[43]

James's answer, then, to the first question he raises as to the "psychogenesis" or origin of ethical beliefs is that they are not the result of the experiences either of the individual or of the race; they are caused by congenital variations which are "accidental" in their first instance (" 'accidental' in the Darwinian sense, as belonging to a cycle of causation inaccessible to the present order of research"[44]), and that these accidental beliefs persevere as a priori postulates which have a natural origin rather than a supernatural one.

A second question that James discusses is what he calls the "metaphysical" question in ethics: What do we mean by the words "good," "evil," and "obligation"? In answering this question in the essay on "The Moral Philosopher and the Moral Life" James argues:

> First of all, it appears that such words can have no application or relevancy in a world in which no sentient life exists. Imagine an absolutely material world, containing only physical and chemical facts, and existing from eternity without a God, without even an interested spectator: would there be any sense in saying of that world that one of its states is better than another? . . . Surely there is no *status* for good and evil to exist in, in a purely insentient world. How can one physical fact, considered simply as a physical fact, be "better" than another? . . . Physical facts simply *are* or are *not;* and neither when present or absent, can they be supposed to make demands. If they do, they can only do so by having desires; and then they have ceased to be purely physical facts, and have become facts of conscious sensibility. Goodness, badness, and obligation must be *realized* somewhere in order really to exist; and the first step in ethical philosophy is to see that no merely inor-

ganic "nature of things" can realize them. Neither moral relations nor the moral law can swing *in vacuo*. Their only habitat can be a mind which feels them; and no world composed of merely physical facts can possibly be a world to which ethical propositions apply.

The moment one sentient being, however, is made a part of the universe, there is a chance for goods and evils really to exist. Moral relations now have their *status,* in that being's consciousness. So far as he feels anything to be good, he makes it good. It *is* good, for him; and being good for him, is absolutely good, for he is the sole creator of values in that universe, and outside of his opinion things have no moral character at all.[45]

Moral relations and moral values do not have their status, then, in some antecedent reality independent of all life. There is an ultimate datum, the valuing of an object by a given consciousness. Beyond this ultimate datum we cannot go: "The philosopher, therefore, . . . must trace the *ought* itself to the *de facto* constitution of some existing consciousness, beyond which, as one of the data of the universe, he as a purely ethical philosopher is unable to go. This consciousness must make the one ideal right by feeling it to be right and the other wrong by feeling it to be wrong."[46]

For many persons the problem of what is right and wrong or good and bad is not a matter of subjective feeling. These matters are to be referred to God, who decides them. But then, *mutatis mutandis,* we have the same argument over again. How does God settle this question? He cannot appeal to some objective moral order outside of his own subjective feelings, for we have just seen that moral orders do not exist independently of a sentient being. "Without a claim actually made by some concrete person there can be no obligation. . . ."[47] God can only appeal to the brute fact that he has certain subjective feelings which he imposes upon us. We tend to think that the claims he makes upon us have some additional validity over and above the fact that he makes them. This validity "rains down upon the claim, we think, from some sublime dimension of being, which the moral law inhabits, much as upon the steel of the compass-needle the influence of the pole rains down from out of the starry heavens. But again, how can an inorganic abstract character of imperativeness, additional to the imperativeness which is in the concrete claim itself, *exist?*"[48]

We simply have, as ultimate data, claims. Whether these claims are human or divine, they have no justification beyond themselves. There is also the further point that "there is some obligation wherever there is a claim."[49]

Take any demand, however slight, which any creature, however weak, may make. Ought it not, for its own sole sake, to be satisfied? If not, prove why not. The only possible kind of proof you could adduce would be the exhibition of another creature who should make a demand that ran the other way. The only possible reason there can be why any phenomenon ought to exist is that such a phenomenon actually is desired.[50]

If we proceed from the base that all demands impose an obligation to be satisfied, we come head on to the third question which James discusses in "The Moral Philosopher and the Moral Life," the casuistic question: What is the order (hierarchy) of goods? If the essence of good is simply to satisfy demands, how do we decide which demands to satisfy? Can we not simply satisfy all

of them? This ideal is impossible of realization in the
world we live in. It is a brute fact of reality that we can
only be in one place at one time; we can only live one
life; if we do one action we must forgo others. A world
in which all of our multitudinous demands could be satisfied would have to be a world, as James points out, of
n-dimensions of space and time. In our one space and one
time we cannot begin to attain the ideal of satisfying all
demands:

> The actually possible in this world is vastly nar-
> rower than all that is demanded; and there is always
> a pinch between the ideal and the actual which can
> only be got through by leaving part of the ideal be-
> hind. . . . So that the ethical philosopher's demand
> for the right scale of subordination in ideals is the
> fruit of an altogether practical need. Some part of
> the ideal must be butchered, and he needs to know
> which part. It is a tragic situation, and no mere spe-
> culative conundrum, with which he has to deal.[51]

If we cannot, then, satisfy all demands, the next best
alternative is to develop a system which will satisfy the
greatest possible number of demands. But how to do this?
Life is a complex and manifold process. Can any philosopher comprehend its richness in such detail as to be
able to see for all persons, with their multitudes of
demands so different from his own, that system which
will best satisfy the greatest possible number of demands?
This is the task of ethical philosophy. But because philosophers are only human, the systems which they project
to accomplish the best of all possible worlds (in a universe in which some worlds are impossible) will often
reflect their own prejudices and inadequacies. In fact,
constructing a theory of ethics will turn out to be much

like constructing any theory. The facts will continually be more complex than the system accounts for. Under these circumstances the only way to construct an adequate theory is by the empirical method. The theorist constructs a theory and then tries it to see how it fits the facts. Where it is a poor fit he or another theorist alters it to seek to include more facts; this process of seeking a better and better theory by experimental testing is the process mankind has gone through in its effort to develop a social system which will be adequate to the satisfaction of as many demands as possible.

The course of history is nothing but the story of men's struggles from generation to generation to find the more and more inclusive order. *Invent some manner* of realizing your own ideals which will also satisfy the alien demands,—that and that only is the path of peace! Following this path, society has shaken itself into one sort of relative equilibrium after another by a series of social discoveries quite analogous to those of science. Polyandry and polygamy and slavery, private warfare and liberty to kill, judicial torture and arbitrary royal power have slowly succumbed to actually aroused complaints; and though some one's ideals are unquestionably the worse off for each improvement, yet a vastly greater total number of them find shelter in our civilized society than in the older savage ways.[52]

And yet if he be a true philosopher he must see that there is nothing final in any actually given equilibrium of human ideals, but that, as our present laws and customs have fought and conquered other past ones, so they will in their turn be overthrown by any newly discovered order which will hush up the com-

see: Discovery of Time

plaints that they still give rise to, without producing others louder still. . . . And although a man always risks much when he breaks away from established rules and strives to realize a larger ideal whole than they permit, yet the philosopher must allow that it is at all times open to any one to make the experiment, provided he fear not to stake his life and character upon the throw. The pinch is always here. Pent in under every system of moral rules are innumerable persons whom it weighs upon, and goods which it represses; and these are always rumbling and grumbling in the background and ready for any issue by which they may get free. . . . These experiments are to be judged, not *a priori,* but by actually finding, after the fact of their making, how much more outcry or how much appeasement comes about. What closet-solutions can possibly anticipate the result of trials made on such a scale? Or what can any superficial theorist's judgment be worth, in a world where every one of hundreds of ideals has its special champion already provided in the shape of some genius expressly born to feel it, and to fight to death in its behalf?[53]

We see, then, that rather than ethics being a deductive process wherein we deduce the moral quality of actions from abstract ethical principles, it is instead an inductive process. By theorizing, experimenting, and retheorizing, we build up by inductive techniques general moral principles from particular ethical observations. "Everywhere the ethical philosopher must wait on facts."[54] And so we are brought back to the point James stated at the beginning of the essay: "There can be no final truth in ethics any more than in physics, until the last man has had his experience and said his say."

James would appear to have answered in an elegant fashion the question as to whether ethics has a natural or a supernatural origin by providing answers to all three of the questions he raises within a naturalistic context: The psychological question is answered by saying that the origin of ethical sensitivities lies in incidental properties which accrued to man in the course of his evolution; the metaphysical question is answered by saying that what we mean by good is the satisfaction of demand, and by evil, the frustration of demand; the casuistic question by saying that human experience has through trial and error developed systems which order goods in a scale determined by the vigor of the complaints received from human beings when their demands are frustrated. In fact, James says in this essay:

> Whether a God exist, or whether no God exist, in yon blue heaven above us bent, we form at any rate an ethical republic here below. And the first reflection which this leads to is that ethics have as genuine and real a foothold in a universe where the highest consciousness is human, as in a universe where there is a God as well. "The religion of humanity" affords a basis for ethics as well as theism does.[55]

But having given us this lucid and straightforward account of a naturalistic ethics, James is unable to leave God out of the picture. In a final section to the essay James says:

> When, however, we believe that a God is there, and that he is one of the claimants, the infinite perspective opens out. The scale of the symphony is incalculably prolonged. The more imperative ideals

now begin to speak with an altogether new objectivity and significance, and to utter the penetrating, shattering, tragically challenging note of appeal. They ring out like the call of Victor Hugo's alpine eagle, "qui parle au precipice et que le gouffre entend," and the strenuous mood awakens at the sound. It saith among the trumpets, ha, ha! it smelleth the battle afar off, the thunder of the captains and the shouting. Its blood is up; and cruelty to the lesser claims, so far from being a deterrent element, does but add to the stern joy with which it leaps to the greater. . . .

The capacity of the strenuous mood lies so deep down among our natural human possibilities that even if there were no metaphysical or traditional grounds for believing in a God, men would postulate one simply as a pretext for living hard, and getting out of the game of existence its keenest possibilities of zest.[56]

The reader must decide for himself whether this is what James has done.

Chapter 3

PRAGMATISM: MEANING AND TRUTH

In the last ten years of his life William James's intellectual interests shifted to a quite different set of philosophical problems and to what might almost be called a second career. Prior to this time he had been known primarily as a psychologist who had some interest in philosophical questions bordering on religion. This first phase of his career began with his *Principles of Psychology* in 1890, continued through *The Will to Believe and Other Essays* in 1897; *Human Immortality: Two Supposed Objections to the Doctrine,* 1898; *Talks to Teachers on Psychology: and to Students on Some of Life's Ideals,* 1899; and culminated in the Gifford Lectures delivered at the University of Edinburgh in 1901-02 and published as *The Varieties of Religious Experience.*

The second phase, which ran from 1902 until his death in 1910, began with a fallow period from 1902 to 1907. During this fallow period he became involved, almost accidentally, in the development of the philosophical movement known as pragmatism. In 1898 James had read an essay before the Philosophical Union at the University of California titled "Philosophical Conceptions and

Practical Results." The University of California printed the essay in *The University Chronicle,* Volume I, pages 287-310, for September, 1898. In this essay James borrowed a doctrine which his friend Charles S. Peirce had developed in the 1870's called "pragmatism" and applied it to the religious problem. Little attention had been paid to Peirce's statement of the doctrine in two essays in *The Popular Science Monthly* for 1877-78, "The Fixation of Belief" and "How to Make Our Ideas Clear," and James's 1898 restatement was generally unnoticed also. However, when James reprinted the essay in a somewhat revised form in *The Journal of Philosophy, Psychology and Scientific Method* (Volume I, pages 673-87) in 1904, under the title "The Pragmatic Method," it aroused considerable comment and launched American pragmatism as a philosophical movement.

With the publication of his book *Pragmatism: A New Name for Some Old Ways of Thinking* in 1907, James became identified as the champion of the new movement. In 1909 he published *The Meaning of Truth: A Sequel to Pragmatism.* The interest in pragmatism led James to an increasing interest in epistemology and metaphysics which resulted in *A Pluralistic Universe* in 1909 and *Essays in Radical Empiricism* in 1912.

Charles Peirce had probably formulated and named the pragmatic doctrine as early as 1872 and had published the first articles about it in 1877-78. James, in his essay on "Philosophical Conceptions and Practical Results," refers to Peirce's early formulation of pragmatism and then states his own slightly more particularized version. Because of its historical interest, and because James never departed significantly from this earliest statement, it may be worthwhile to quote the opening paragraphs of this essay:

I will seek to define with you merely what seems to be the most likely direction in which to start upon the trail of truth. Years ago this direction was given to me by an American philosopher whose home is in the East, and whose published works, few as they are and scattered in periodicals, are not fit expression of his powers. I refer to Mr. Charles S. Peirce, with whose very existence as a philosopher I dare say many of you are unacquainted. He is one of the most original of contemporary thinkers; and the principle of practicalism—or pragmatism, as he called it, when I first heard him enunciate it at Cambridge in the early '70's—is the clue or compass by following which I find myself more and more confirmed in believing we may keep our feet upon the proper trail.

Peirce's principle, as we may call it, may be expressed in a variety of ways, all of them very simple. In *The Popular Science Monthly* for January, 1878, he introduces it as follows: The soul and meaning of thought, he says, can never be made to direct itself towards anything but the production of belief, belief being the demicadence which closes a musical phrase in the symphony of our intellectual life. Thought in movement has thus for its only possible motive the attainment of thought at rest. But when our thought about an object has found its rest in belief, then our action on the subject can firmly and safely begin. Beliefs, in short, are really rules for action; and the whole function of thinking is but one step in the production of habits of action. If there were any part of a thought that made no difference in the thought's practical consequences, then that part would be no proper element of the thought's significance. Thus the same thought may be clad in different words; but if the different words suggest no different conduct, they are mere outer accretions, and have no part in the thought's meaning. If, however, they determine conduct differently, they are essential elements of the significance. "Please open the door," and *"veuillez ouvrir la porte,"* in French, mean just the same thing; but "D——n you, open the door," although in English, *means* something very different. Thus to develop a thought's meaning we need only determine what conduct it is fitted to produce; that conduct is for us its sole significance. And the tangible fact at the root of all our thought-distinctions, however subtle, is that there is no one of them so fine as to consist in anything but a possible difference of practice. To attain perfect clearness in our thoughts of an object, then, we need only consider what effects of a conceivably practical kind the object may involve—what sensations we are to expect from it, and what reactions we must prepare. Our conception of these effects, then, is for us the whole of our conception of the object, so far as that conception has positive significance at all.

This is the principle of Peirce, the principle of pragmatism. I think myself that it should be expressed more broadly than Mr. Peirce expresses it. The ultimate test for us of what a truth means is indeed the conduct it dictates or inspires. But it inspires that conduct because it first foretells some particular turn to our experience which shall call for just that conduct from us. And I should prefer for our purposes this evening to express Peirce's principle by saying that the effective meaning of any philosophical proposition can always be brought down to some particular consequence, in our future practical experience, whether active or passive; the point lying rather in the fact that the experience must be particular than in the fact that it must be active.

To take in the importance of this principle, one must get accustomed to applying it to concrete cases. Such use as I am able to make of it convinces me that to be mindful of it in philosophical disputations tends wonderfully to smooth out misunderstandings and to bring in peace. If it did nothing else, then, it would yield a sovereignly valuable rule of method for discussion. So I shall devote the rest of this precious hour with you to its elucidation, because I sincerely think that if you once grasp it, it will shut your steps out from many an old false opening, and head you in the true direction for the trail.

One of its first consequences is this. Suppose there are two different philosophical definitions, or propositions, or maxims, or what not, which seem to contradict each other, and about which men dispute. If, by supporting the truth of the one, you can foresee no conceivable practical consequence to anybody at any time or place, which is different from what you would foresee if you supposed the truth of the other, why then the difference between the two propositions is no difference—it is only a specious and verbal difference, unworthy of further contention. Both formulas mean radically the same thing, although they may say it in such different words. It is astonishing to see how many philosophical disputes collapse into insignificance the moment you subject them to this simple test. There can be no difference which doesn't make a difference —no difference in abstract truth which does not express itself in a difference of concrete fact, and of conduct consequent upon the fact, imposed on somebody, somehow, somewhere, and somewhen. It is true that a certain shrinkage of values often seems to occur in our general formulas when we measure their meaning in this prosaic and practical way. They diminish. But the vastness that is merely based on vagueness is a false appearance of importance, and not a vastness worth retaining. The x's, y's, and z's always do shrivel, as I have heard a learned friend say, whenever at the end of your algebraic computation they change into so many plain a's, b's and c's—but the whole function of algebra is, after all, to get them into that more definite shape; and the whole function of philosophy ought to be to find out what definite difference it will make to you and me, at definite instants of our life, if this world-formula or that world-formula be the one which is true.[1]

The heart of this statement is the principle "that the effective meaning of any philosophical proposition can always be brought down to some particular consequence, in our future practical experience, whether active or passive; the point lying rather in the fact that the experience must be particular than in the fact that it must be active."

We may begin by inquiring into some of the basic concepts referred to in this principle. The first such concept is the term "meaning." What is a meaning? To borrow the title of a well-known book in this field, what is "the meaning of meaning"? When we talk about a meaning are we talking about a mental image, a set of written words, or a vocal utterance? A little consideration will suggest that we do not mean any of these. The rather common notion that the meaning of a term is the mental image it produces is dispelled by the contemplation of the fact that no mental image accompanies our more complex thought processes. (The reader is invited to ask himself what mental image is produced in his mind by the statement that "no mental image accompanies our more complex thought processes.") No mental images are relevant to the meaning of "Eternal vigilance is the price of liberty" or "Love makes the world go around," to suggest two examples taken at random.

In a somewhat similar way it may be seen that the meaning of a statement cannot be a set of words, whether written or spoken. The most obvious refutation of this notion is suggested by the fact that the same meaning may be conveyed by quite different words, as when translating from one language to another. *Es regnet, il pleut,* and *it is raining* all express the same meaning, but the words are obviously different—so that the meaning cannot be identified with the words.

Another difficulty arises from the fact that words which are the vehicle for conveying meanings, although they are not *themselves* meanings, are used to convey many major kinds of meanings. For our purposes we may indicate these kinds as the ceremonial, emotive, and cognitive uses of words or languages. In the "ceremonial" use of language we are using words with no intent that they should be taken literally. A major portion of our day-to-day use of language comes in this category. Remarks about the weather, greetings, and farewells all come in this class. In the "emotive" use of language our concern is with the expression of emotion; thus if someone steps on my toe and I say "ouch!" I am not engaging in a ceremony or describing my feelings; I am expressing them. Finally, whenever we do undertake to describe some fact about ourselves or the world around us, we intend to communicate to someone else our intellectual understanding of a situation. Such a usage is called the cognitive use of language.

To illustrate these usages, if I meet you on the street and say, "How are you?" I am using language in its cere- monial function. I don't really want to know the state of your health. No matter how poorly you may feel, the appropriate ceremonial reply is "Fine." If you see an old friend you have not seen for many years you may exclaim with joy, "How *are* you?" In this case you do not intend to simply engage in a greeting ceremony, but rather to express your great pleasure at the sight of an old acquaintance. Finally, if you went to your doctor's office and he inquired of you, "How are you?" and you replied, "Fine," when you in fact had sundry ills, you would miss the point of the whole proceedings.

In the above examples the same words were used for quite different purposes. This ambiguity makes it neces- sary to state which of these three linguistic functions we are concerned with in our quest for the meaning of a term. Although each of them has points of philosophical interest, pragmatism as a theory of meaning is concerned primarily with the cognitive use of language—the intel- lectual meaning, the descriptive meaning, or what is sometimes called the scier ific meaning. If we reply to our doctor's inquiry by saying that we are fine, what "knowledge" are we seeking to convey?

We may then narrow our search for the nature of meaning. We are not, in the present context, pursuing emotive or ceremonial meanings but cognitive meanings. We have seen that a cognitive meaning is neither a set of words nor a set of images. What then is it?

We are moving, with this question, into a branch of philosophy known traditionally as epistemology. Epis- temology is the study of the nature and origin of knowl- edge. It seeks answers to such questions as: what kind of thing is an idea, where do ideas come from, what rela- tions do our ideas bear to the world outside of our minds?

Traditionally epistemology has established certain alternatives which recognize basically different approaches to these questions. One might say, for example, that all knowledge comes from—or could come from—reason alone. One who held such a view would be called a rationalist in epistemology. Or one could hold that sense experience—seeing, hearing, touching, tasting, etc.—is the sole source of knowledge. In such a case he would be an empiricist. In general in the history of philosophy, those who have had a strong mathematical bent—Plato, Descartes, Spinoza, Leibniz—have tended to some form of rationalism. Those with a strong scientific bent—Democritus, Aristotle, David Hume, John Stuart Mill—have leaned toward some form of empiricism.

James comes in the latter group. He dedicated his book on pragmatism "To the memory of John Stuart Mill from whom I first learned the pragmatic openness of mind and whom my fancy likes to picture as our leader were he alive today." He often described his position as "radical empiricism" and used this phrase in the title of one of his books. With what James thought of as "open-mindedness" and his critics as equivocation, he held, in a separate mental compartment from his empiricism, to some beliefs about the existence of God and the possibility of communicating with disembodied spirits which many empiricists would view with a jaundiced eye.

Nevertheless, in his technical philosophy he was an empiricist. His empiricism differed significantly from that of earlier empiricists, however. Traditionally, empiricism had answered questions about the origin of knowledge by saying that knowledge originated in sense experiences. Empiricists had answered questions about the nature of knowledge by saying that knowledge consisted of the calling up in memory of recollections of past experiences. For the pragmatists this was not enough. Knowledge was not simply the passive process of looking back on past experience; knowledge—for Peirce and James and Dewey —was the active projection of experience into the future. It was the projection onto an anticipated situation, the imaginative reconstruction of an as yet unexperienced situation in terms of past experiences but in terms which proposed future solutions to a present problem in a new alternative. This emphasis on the projection of experience into the future so that knowledge performed the function of providing a guide to action was the characteristic feature from which all the unique elements of pragmatism were to flow.

What John Dewey has called this "prospective" orientation in pragmatism as distinguished from the "retrospective" orientation of earlier empiricisms is indicated by James in the passage quoted at the beginning of this chapter when he says that a meaning inspires conduct, "But it inspires that conduct because it first *foretells* some particular turn to our experience which shall call for just that conduct from us." (Italics supplied.)

In discussing James's development of pragmatism, Dewey wrote: "Pragmatism, thus, presents itself as an extension of historical empiricism with the fundamental difference that it does not insist upon antecedent phenomena but upon consequent phenomena; not upon the precedents but upon the possibilities of action, and this change in point of view is almost revolutionary in its consequences."[2]

It is not, I think, any exaggeration to describe this change in orientation as "revolutionary." James had written as early as 1875 that "The truth of a thing or idea is its meaning, or its destiny, that which grows out of it. This would be a doctrine reversing the opinion of the empiricists that the meaning of an idea is that which it has grown from."[3]

A second basic element in James's empiricism was a major consequence of this reorientation of thought from the past to the future. If ideas are projected into the future, it is requisite that the mind actively operate upon its ideas so as to project them into a future which is never quite like the past. It selects among its ideas, it reorganizes and reconstructs. It *acts* upon them so as to create from its present ideas a guide to the future which will seek to assure experiences which it desires and to repress those it wishes to avoid.

In this process the mind is not the passive recipient of sense experiences—Locke's *tabula rasa*. The mind is active in the imaginative reconstruction of the past to anticipate new possibilities in the future. This active role of mind, or of "thinking," was quite a new departure from the traditional empiricist notion which Dewey called "the spectator theory of knowledge" and which saw the mind as a mere passive recipient of sensory experiences.

The active projection of experience into the future is common to the pragmatism of Peirce and James and Dewey. It is what Peirce meant by his description of an idea as a "plan for action." It led Dewey to adopt the term "instrumentalism" for his version of pragmatism in order to emphasize the role of thought as an instrument for developing imaginative possibilities for solving anticipated problems.

Dewey refers to:

. . . one phase of the philosophy of William James, namely, that validity is not a matter of origin nor of antecedents, but of consequents. This statement, associated with the philosophy of all pragmatism, is often treated as if it were directed merely against previous rationalisms. Its more direct objective of attack is previous empiricisms. . . . The whole point of James's philosophy, which comes out better in some chapters of his *Psychology,* I think, especially in the last chapter of the second volume, than in his lectures on *Pragmatism,* is that the value of ideas is independent of their origin, that it is a matter of their outcome as they are used in directing new observation and new experience.[4]

This notion of an idea as a way of actively questioning the objective world is marked by Perry as distinguishing James's position from traditional empiricism.

Experience is authoritative in both cases, but whereas according to the traditional view experience *has* spoken, according to James's view experience has yet to speak, and its response will be proportional to the boldness and happy inspiration with which it is interrogated. The truly empirical mind is not the mind which yields to habit or passively accepts its own history as a revelation of existence, but the mind which imagines curious possibilities and gives nature every chance to reveal itself in unfamiliar ways.[5]

And so we begin to come in sight of some of what James intends by "meaning" of an idea. We get as a first approximation that the meaning of an idea is that imaginative reconstruction of past experience which is projected as a guide for future action.

If we say that the meaning of an idea lies in its implications for the future, a number of questions raise themselves. Among all the kinds of implications for the future which an idea may have, which ones are we to single out as its meanings? Are we, for instance, to concern ourselves with its implications for other people, or for generations yet unborn, or for ourselves? Are we to concern ourselves with its speculative, theoretical, or practical implications? Are we to concern ourselves with its general implications or its particular ones? Are we to concern ourselves with its implications for logical reason or sensory experience? These and a host of other problems arise to plague us.

We may make an approach to them by an examination of some of James's psychological analyses on this point. It would be strange indeed if such a distinguished psychologist as James should hold a view about the meaning of ideas without developing it from a psychological base. James does, in fact, hold some psychological views which are quite relevant to his epistemological ones.

It may be appropriate to begin by outlining briefly the distinction between the interest of a psychologist in ideas and that of an epistemologist. To oversimplify, we may say that the two basic elements in the knowledge situation are the knower and the known. Most commonly this means some knowing mind which knows some external physical world. In this situation there is a mind to be studied and a physical world to be studied. The study of the mind and its processes is the business of the psychologist; the study of the physical world and its processes is the business of the physical scientist. We thus have two entities studied by two separate disciplines. We may now ask: what is the relation between them? How are the mind and the physical world related? Does mind affect the world, and does the world affect the mind? Does the mind know the world exactly as it really is, or only dimly and inaccurately? Is the world of the physicist really objective or is it colored by the mind through which he looks at it? These and many other questions about the relation of the mind to the physical world do not properly fall within psychology as the study of mental behavior, or within physics as the study of physical behavior. They are problems in epistemology, which seeks to answer the question about the relation of the subjective mind to the objective world. It is this effort to bridge what James called "the epistemological gulf," the empty space between mind and world, which characterizes the discipline of epistemology, or theory of knowledge.

In an effort to reach James's answers to the epistemological question we may begin by a brief statement of his psychological view on the role of ideas in human behavior.

James expressed his position as early as 1881 when, in an essay titled "Reflex Action and Theism," he wrote:

There is no one of those complicated performances in the convolutions of the brain to which our trains of thought correspond, which is not a mere middle term interposed between an incoming sensation that arouses it and an outgoing discharge of some sort, inhibitory if not exciting, to which itself gives rise. The structural unit of the nervous system is in fact a triad, neither of whose elements has any independent existence. The sensory impression exists only for the sake of awaking the central process of reflection, and the central process of reflection exists only for the sake of calling forth the final act. All action is thus reaction upon the outer world; and the middle stage of consideration or contemplation or thinking is only a place of transit, the bottom of a loop, both of whose ends have their point of application in the outer world. If it should ever happen that it led to no active measures, it would fail of its essential function, and would have to be considered either pathological or abortive. The current of life which runs in at our eyes or ears is meant to run out at hands, feet, or lips. The only use of the thoughts it occasions while inside is to determine its direction to whichever of these organs shall, on the whole, under the circumstances actually present, act in the way most propitious to our welfare.[6]

We may represent this paragraph diagrammatically in the following fashion:

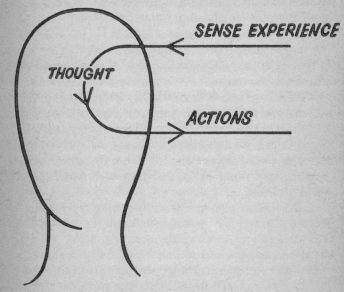

An examination of this diagram will serve to show why, when James formulated his version of pragmatism, he defined it as the doctrine that "To attain perfect clearness in our thoughts of an object, then, we need only consider . . . what sensations we are to expect from it and what reactions we must prepare."

Thus, one knows what he means by (i.e., what his thought is of) an apple, if he knows what sense experiences he will get from an apple and what actions he will engage in toward any object he will call an apple.

Of the two classes of elements that went into a "meaning"—sensations and reactions—James tended to stress the latter, the action component. He says in the 1881 essay: "The willing [acting] department of our nature, in short, dominates both the conceiving [thinking] department and the feeling [perceiving] department; or, in plainer English, perception and thinking are only there for behavior's sake."[7]

This orientation toward behavior, the way in which we act, as the primary interpretant of our ideas was the aspect of meaning which James wished to stress by using the word "practical." He meant it in the sense of our "practice" or behavior toward an object; the sense in which a doctor has a "practice," or a pianist "practices," or we talk about something as a "bad practice." His critics, however, persisted in interpreting it as meaning that sense of "practical" in which the worldly and common-sense moneymaking attitude is opposed to the theoretical and philosophical.

James says that he is not ruling out the theoretical, but only the speculative, which does not affect our practice in any way:

> One can easily get into a verbal mess at this point, and my own experience with "pragmatism" makes me shrink from the dangers that lie in the word "practical" . . . I am quite willing . . . to ascribe a primarily theoretical function to our intellect, provided you on your part then agree to discriminate "theoretic" or scientific knowledge from the deeper "speculative" knowledge aspired to by most philosophers.[8]

Thus the meaning of an idea is to be interpreted as the ways in which it influences our practice or our behavior.

Finally, it would not do to simply state these practices in general terms. They had to be stated specifically. The idea involved an active component—where we were reacting to the idea—and a passive component—where we were receiving certain sense experiences. But "whether active or passive . . . the experience must be particular." It is not adequate to simply describe a chair as an object one can sit upon. After all, it is possible to sit upon a table or on the floor. A chair is an object one would look for if he were preparing to sit down (in preference to a table or the floor), if he did not see a chair he might search for one, or, *in extremis,* build one, and he would expect that sitting upon a chair would provide a greater sense of comfort than sitting upon the table or floor.

These consequences in action of our having a certain idea influence our practice. If we have the idea something is a chair we act differently toward it than if we have the idea it is a bed of nails. These consequences for practice of an idea were called, by James, the practical consequences of the idea. We thus reach the formulation of the pragmatic doctrine which defines the meaning of an idea as the sum of its practical consequences.

All of this gives us a definition of the pragmatic doctrine as the belief that the cognitive meaning of an idea consists in knowing the sum of the consequences in practice of that idea, that is, the sum of the sense experiences we would expect and the actions we would be prepared to execute toward any object to which we would apply that idea.

Thus to any object to which we are prepared to apply the idea of "apple" there are certain practical consequences we would expect—certain particular sense experiences we would expect from the object and certain particular actions we would be prepared to perform toward the object. These are not the same sense experiences we would expect from an object we would call a "pear," nor the same actions we would perform in dealing with a pear.

Thus we can tell what a man's idea of an "apple" is by having him indicate the sense experiences he would expect and the actions he would prepare. And we can see what he means by a "pear" by seeing what differences in sense experiences and actions there are for him between "pears" and "apples." If the two sets of practical consequences are identical, then there is no difference in what he means by "pear" and "apple." ". . . the tangible fact at the root of all our thought-distinctions, however subtle, is that there is no one of them so fine as to consist in anything but a possible difference of practice."

Finally, if an individual is unable to specify any possible practical consequences which would ensue from his idea, then the idea is empty. It is without meaning, or meaningless.

It is astonishing to see how many philosophical disputes collapse into insignificance the moment you subject them to this simple test of tracing a concrete consequence. There can *be* no difference anywhere that doesn't *make* a difference elsewhere—no difference in abstract truth that doesn't express itself in a difference in concrete fact and in conduct consequent upon that fact, imposed on somebody, somehow, somewhere and somewhen.[9]

If pragmatism is the theory that the meaning of an idea consists in the sum of the ways in which the idea influences our behavior, we may apply this theory to different ideas to see what they mean. It is not so difficult to apply it to our ideas of concrete physical objects. Thus we may see how one could list the sense experiences he would expect and the reaction he would prepare for any object he would call a chair, or an apple or a tree. But what about abstract ideas? How does one ascertain the sense experiences and actions relevant to them? Concepts such as justice, truth, goodness, beauty, and reality seem to be more difficult to deal with. James's most persistent and systematic effort lay in his concern with applying the pragmatic theory of meaning to ascertain the meaning of the term "truth." In doing so he developed what came to be called "the pragmatic theory of truth."

In the nineteenth century there were many thinkers for whom truth was spelled with a capital T. Truth had a halo about it. It was the capstone of human knowledge and human endeavor. To reduce its meaning to something as mundane as the ways in which we behaved in practice was to degrade "truth" and to dissipate its greatest values. Accordingly James's efforts to define truth in terms of its practical consequences met with a good deal of opposition.

We may approach this problem by asking what kind of thing truth is. There are many persons for whom the words "true" and "real" are synonymous. So that, for them, to say that something is true or to say that it is real is to say the same thing about it. Such usage would allow us to talk about a "true fact" and a "real fact" as being the same thing. But if we use these terms in this way, one of them is superfluous. To avoid redundancy we must ascribe a usage to one of them which does not belong to the other.

In the knowledge process, there is an idea in the mind which "knows" an object in the physical world. Better usage than that described above will use the term "real" to refer to the object and the term "true" (or "false") to apply to the idea. Thus we say of objects of knowledge which actually exist in the external world—like trees and chairs and houses—that they are real. Objects of knowledge which do not exist—like unicorns and fairies—are said to be unreal or to be fictitious in nature. Thus "reality" is a property of objects. It is that property they have when they actually exist in the external world.

Truth, on the other hand, is a property of our ideas about the object. If the idea is a correct idea of the object, we say it is a true idea. If it is incorrect we say that it is false. That truth is not the same thing as reality may be seen from the fact that we may have true ideas of things which are not real. Thus if your idea of a unicorn is that it is an animal the size of a small horse with a single horn protruding from the center of its forehead, your idea is true, even though unicorns are not real.

In seeking to discover what kind of thing truth is, we see, first of all, then, that it is a property of our ideas, not of the objects in the world. We may then ask: of the many properties which ideas may have, which one of them is it that makes for truth or falsity?

There were two leading theories of truth prior to James's pragmatic theory. One of these was the coherence theory of truth. This theory said that an idea was true if it had the property of "cohering" with other ideas, already known to be true. The notion was that the whole body of truths would demonstrate a consistency, they would not contradict one another. Thus an idea that was consistent with them would be apt to be true, an idea that was not consistent with them would be apt to be false. This theory actually made truth a property of the relation between ideas rather than a relation between an idea and its object.

The second theory of truth made the property of truth a property which the idea had if it stood in a certain relation to the object it was about. This relation was described variously as "copying" or "corresponding" to the object. This copy theory of truth or correspondence theory of truth defined truth as that property an idea had if it "copied" or "corresponded with" the object. James considered the pragmatic theory of truth to be a version of this latter theory.

He got to the pragmatic theory of truth by applying the pragmatic theory of meaning to the notion of "corresponds with." What does it mean to say an idea "corresponds with" an object? This is not as simple a question as it may seem to be. Suppose you have an idea of a table in your mind. Let us represent your idea by the symbol †. Suppose there to be in the external world a table to which you wish to compare your idea to see if they correspond. Let us represent the table by the symbol ‡. How can we ascertain whether or not † is a copy of (i.e., corresponds with) ‡? We cannot take the idea out of the mind and lay it on the table to see if there is a one-to-one correspondence between them. We cannot bring the table into the mind for such a purpose either. We can look at the table and examine it carefully. If we do we will develop a second idea $†^2$. We can compare our first idea $†^1$ with the second idea $†^2$, but this is not what we want. We want to compare $†^1$ with ‡! If we compare $†^1$ with $†^2$ we may find a correspondence. But we have at the best here only established a coherence theory of truth—two ideas agree with one another. We can say that $†^1$ corresponds with ‡ if we can show that $†^1$ corresponds with $†^2$ and $†^2$ corresponds with ‡. But how can we do this latter task? To find out if ‡ corresponds to $†^2$ is only our original problem over once again; we look carefully at ‡ and get another idea $†^3$; we can compare $†^2$ with $†^3$, but we are still without any means for establishing that $†^3$ is a copy of the table. Thus if by being true we mean to say that an idea is a copy of, or corresponds with, an external object, there is no way to establish that the idea corresponds in any simple way.

James suggested a pragmatic alternative. If the idea corresponded with the object, would there, perhaps, be, among the consequences of the idea in practice (i.e., when acted upon), a consequence which would be present when the idea was true (i.e., corresponded with the object) that would not be found when the idea was false, or did not correspond? When the matter is put this way we see immediately that there is one such significant consequence. If the idea is acted upon and corresponds with the object, then, in practice, the idea will work in dealing with the object. If the idea is acted upon and it does not correspond with the object, then, in practice, it will not work in dealing with the object. Accordingly, James defines "corresponding with" pragmatically as the property an idea has when it works as a means of dealing with an object. Thus our idea of an object is true if the idea works in dealing with the object. To find out if the idea is true we put it to the test to see if it works. This process of testing the idea is what the scientist calls verifying it. So, says James, the truth of an idea is its verification process. The idea literally becomes true in the process of verification.

This reduction of truth to its practical success in dealing with the world—what James called the "cash value" of the idea—offended those for whom the truth was a noble abstraction. Against them James waged a vigorous polemic.

In the chapter titled "Pragmatism's Conception of Truth" in his book *Pragmatism,* James wrote that "First, you know, a new theory is attacked as absurd; then it is admitted to be true, but obvious and insignificant; finally it is seen to be so important that its adversaries claim that they themselves discovered it."[10] In this chapter he goes on to describe the pragmatic theory of truth in these words:

> Truth . . . is a property of certain of our ideas. It means their "agreement" as falsity means their disagreement with "reality." Pragmatists and intellectualists both accept this definition as a matter of course. They begin to quarrel only after the question is raised as to what may precisely be meant by the term "agreement," and what by the term "reality" when reality is taken as something for our ideas to agree with. . . .
>
> . . . The great assumption of the intellectualists is that truth means essentially an inert static relation. When you've got your true idea of anything, there's an end of the matter. You're in possession, you know . . . and nothing more need follow on that climax of your rational destiny. Epistemologically you are in stable equilibrium.
>
> Pragmatism, on the other hand, asks its usual question. "Grant an idea or belief to be true," it says, "what concrete difference will its being true make in any one's actual life; how will the truth be realized? What experiences will be different from those which should obtain if the belief were false? What, in short, is the truth's cash-value in experiential terms?"
>
> The moment pragmatism asks this question, it sees the answer: *True ideas are those that we can assimilate, validate, corroborate and verify. False ideas are those that we can not.* That is the practical difference it makes to us to have true ideas; that, therefore, is the meaning of truth, for it is all that truth is known as.[11]

What constitutes the verification, the workingness of an idea? We have seen earlier that an idea is a prediction of certain future expected sense experiences correlated with certain forms of action on our part. The correlation is of this order, that an idea is an expectation that if we act in a certain manner toward an object to which this idea is applicable, then we will experience a certain predicted sense experience. Thus my idea of an apple is, in part, that if I act so as to bite any object that is an apple, that I will have sense experiences of "crunchiness" and "apple taste."

If I say of an object X that "X is an apple," this statement is verified (found to be true) if, upon biting the apple, I have the predicted sense experiences. A true idea is one, then, that leads us successfully to certain predicted experiences; false ideas do not. This notion of "successful-leading" is identical with "truth" for James.

If we carefully consider this notion that truth is a property exhibited by any idea that leads us successfully in dealing with experiences of objects, we may notice some of the paradoxes of the pragmatic theory of truth. One of these is that if truth is a property of our ideas, then it would follow that where there are no ideas there is no truth. In 1915 Einstein announced in the Special Theory of Relativity that the speed of light was a limiting velocity for objects traveling with a uniform velocity in relation to one another. James's theory of truth requires us to say that it was not true that the velocity of light was a limiting velocity before Einstein announced it. The reason for this is that no one had this as an idea and therefore no one could have had it as a true idea. It may have been a "real fact" that the velocity of light was a limiting velocity, but it was not a "true idea." This queer way of talking follows from the distinction between truth as a property of ideas and "reality" as a property of objects.

It is easy to see from this analysis how truth will grow and change. As new ideas about the limiting velocities of objects are developed and verified, they will be added to our truths about such matters and the truth will change. "The truth of an idea is not a stagnant property inherent in it. Truth *happens* to an idea. It *becomes* true, is *made* true by events."[12]

It follows, further, from this that there is no absolute truth. We never know what new ideas about an object tomorrow will bring. If these ideas are verified they add to the truth about it. Even though we may now know all that ever will be known about something, we can't know that that is the case. No absolute truth can be known until no further experience can be had. "The 'absolutely' true, meaning what no further experience will ever alter, is that ideal vanishing-point towards which we imagine that all our temporary truths will some day converge."[13]

The surrender of a belief in absolute truth was another of the aspects of James's position that so irked those who disagreed with him. There is a feeling on the part of many people that there are only two choices in the truth process. Either there is absolute truth or there is no truth at all. The notion of a "relative truth" sounds to them like a contradiction in terms. Since James believed that truth was relative—and since he taught this in all areas of knowledge including ethics and religion—it may be helpful to examine his position.

The position of the absolutist is that there are certain truths which are absolute—i.e., are the same for all persons at all times and under all circumstances. These truths can be known and, furthermore, we can know that we know them. Thus the absolutist will hold that he knows certain truths which will be the same for all persons at all times and under all circumstances.

James believes the position of the absolutist to be a dogmatic one—a position for which no justification can be given. He held this position because he believed that whenever in the history of thought a proposition has been asserted to be absolute it has turned out to be one of two types. One type is empty of meaning and hence says nothing, as for example, $2+2=4$. This statement does not have either truth or falsity without our specifying two of what plus two of what. Two apples plus two apples equal four apples. But two lighted matches plus two sticks of dynamite equal one explosion. Of course, we are told that we can't add matches to dynamite. Careful examination of the rules under which addition is permissible turns out to show, however, that the rules are defined so as to allow us to add only things which, when added, give the right answer—thus, by definition, if two of a certain object plus two others don't give four, they can't properly be added. This makes $2+2=4$ true by definition. Such rules do not tell us anything about the world—since we do not know what objects can be added until we try them and see if they produce the right answers. The rules are empty of content so far as the world is concerned. Being empty, they say nothing. Saying nothing, they can never be false. Since they are never false, they are considered absolutely true. But their truth comes solely because they are defined so as to rule out all cases that would falsify them. Philosophers have recognized for some time now, and James was among the first to do so, that such statements are definitions only. They tell how we have resolved to use words. They do not tell anything about the world, but only about us.

The second type of absolute proposition is the one that means too much. It is, so to speak, a different thing for all men. Both the United States and the U.S.S.R. describe themselves as believing in democracy, but they mean quite different things by it. For hundreds of years scientists have believed in atoms, but the atom of Democritus was quite different from that of Newton or Rutherford or Bohr. Thus it is correct to say that scientists have believed in atoms for centuries only if we allow the word to mean quite different things in different centuries.

Religious and moral absolutes suffer from these same difficulties. "All men believe that God is good and sin is evil" is true in both senses that it allows by definition only good things to be attributes of God and only evil things to be sin, and different men at different times and under different circumstances have meant quite different things by "God" and "sin," so that the apparent absoluteness of words such as these is only a cloak hiding a relativism of meanings.

The only alternative that many people see, when faced with the difficulties of absolutism, is skepticism. The skeptic holds that there is no truth at all, or, if there is, we cannot know it. James could not subscribe to this view either. As we have seen above (p. 50), he explicitly repudiates it as a possible position in philosophy.

The absolutist-skeptic dichotomy holds to the view that you either know something or you don't know it. Now, these are not the only two alternatives. You may know it approximately.

Thus a man who wants to get from Boston to New York may not know exactly where New York is, still he may know approximately. He may know that it is south of Boston, for example. Or he may know that it is on the Atlantic coast somewhere. Or he may know it is within a circle of five hundred miles radius. Given any of these pieces of knowledge, and time enough, he will eventually find New York.

This kind of approach to knowledge which proceeds by trial and error, by experimentation, and by exhausting alternatives is in a crude sense the method of science—the so-called empirical method. This is the method James would have us adhere to.

The analogy with the search for New York is not exactly appropriate in that the scientist does not know whether there is any answer to his questions (i.e., whether there is a city called New York), and he never finds signposts saying "City Limits of New York," that is, he never knows that he has actually arrived at his goal. Tomorrow may bring some unexpected bit of knowledge which will show that he is not yet there.

However, the empirical method cannot be conducted from a skeptical base. If the scientist believes that there is no truth, then he won't look for it, and if he doesn't look for it, he won't find it even if it does exist. This would be irrational. This would be like the man lost in the forest who says there is no way out and sits down to await death by starvation. There may not be any way out, but if there is a way, it will only be found by looking for it. Therefore it is unreasonable not to look. Hence James rejects skepticism because it is irrational, it says there is no use looking, it closes off inquiry and prevents our finding an answer if there is an answer to be found. In James's view no method is rational which "blocks the road to inquiry," which prevents us from finding an answer if there is an answer to be found. He therefore rejects absolutism because it is dogmatic and skepticism because it is irrational.

The empiricist, however, cannot justify his position either. And James sees this. The empiricist commits an act of faith. He believes there are answers to our questions and that by looking we can come closer and closer to them and that we can eventually find them. But he does not know this, for no absolute answer has ever been found. Or, if it has, we do not know this absolutely, for tomorrow has a habit of refuting our most firmly established theories.

Empiricism gives us answers which are not absolute; they are relative. They are relative to the best evidence we have been able to gather up to this point in our inquiry. We therefore hold to them tentatively and subject to further correction. Truth in this sense is not something absolute, it is a working hypothesis. Acting on it, we move into the future. If the hypothesis is wrong we will find out and be able to correct it. If it guides us aright this time that is one more bit of evidence in its favor. But the skeptic who does not formulate any hypotheses can never correct them by the discovery of errors or reinforce them by the act of having them lead him successfully.

This act of faith—the belief that there are answers and we can find them—is intrinsic to all of James's philosophy. He insists upon an element of belief—over and above what we can prove rationally or experimentally—in all of the knowledge process. This is the argument he pursues in the essay on "The Will to Believe," for example. In this essay he classifies the agnostic in religion with the skeptic in knowledge. It is traditional to find two alternatives in religion: the theist, who knows there is a God, and the atheist, who knows there is not. Thomas Henry Huxley sought to invent a third position. Both the theist and the atheist are "gnostics": they claim to know. They claim there is evidence which is sufficient to render a verdict one way or the other. But the "agnostic" is a not-knower. He may know the arguments but he does not find them conclusive in either direction, and so he stays in a state of suspended judgment, not knowing which way to go.

James excoriates agnosticism. He says that there are two truth values not ordinarily kept separate but which are relevant to agnosticism. One of the values we expect from knowing the truth is that we will avoid error. If we know New York to be south of us we will be able to avoid the error of going north. A second value is that of knowing the truth, that is, knowing how to get to New York. The agnostic is so enamored of the first value, i.e., so desirous of avoiding error, that he forever shuts himself off from the second value, knowing the truth. By committing himself to not going in any direction at all he does not take the wrong road, but neither will he ever find the right road. In refusing to exercise our will, in refusing to believe, we avoid error, but we also lose the right ever to know the truth. For truth is only discovered by those who have the courage to act on their beliefs and to put them to the test.

In addition to this there is the added difficulty in religion that agnosticism is not only irrational but it is also perilous, for if religion is true and if we accept it, we gain a happiness now which is lost to us forever in the agnostic view. Because James holds that an element of belief is essential to the knowledge process, he adjures us to believe a position based on our desires whenever knowledge and experience are unable to decide an issue for us, and so he gets to the first step on the route which will allow him to reconcile his scientific empiricism with a religious supernaturalism.

Since empiricism requires an act of faith at the beginning (the belief that answers are possible and we can find them) and often also at the acting end (the arguments are not conclusive either way, so that if we act we act on faith) let us then believe, in these latter cases, in the kind of world we would like to be living in, so that if our lives are going to be an experiment testing one or the other alternatives, let them at least be tests of the alternative we would find emotionally the most satisfying if it were to turn out to be true.

Not only in religion but also in morals we are told that a commitment beyond knowledge is necessary. "There is but one unconditional commandment, which is that we should seek incessantly, with fear and trembling, so to vote and act as to bring about the very largest total universe of good which we can see."[14] The "fear and trembling" come because we do not know that our actions will bring about the total good; we act on faith in the hope that they will.

On the whole, the problem of the meaning of "truth" turned out to be a much more subtle, difficult, and complicated problem than it had appeared to be at first sight. It was one thing to say that "true ideas work"—a statement which most philosophers would probably find palatable; it was another to say "the truth of an idea consists in its workability"—a statement which denigrated truth too much for most of James's contemporaries; and it was still worse to say, as James did, that "any idea that works is true."

This latter statement was logically required by James's definition of truth. If "truth" is to be defined as "workability," then the two are synonymous; therefore whenever one would use "truth" he could substitute "workability," and conversely. One might protest—as James's critics did —that things could work without necessarily being true. It might "work" for certain purposes for me to believe that I was Napoleon, but this would not make it true that I was. It "worked" in the thirteenth century to believe that the earth was flat. Are we to infer that it is true that the

earth was flat in the thirteenth century—and that it became round when Columbus and Magellan sailed around
it? The Ptolemaic theory, Euclidean space, and New-
tonian physics all "worked" at one time.

These criticisms did not cause James to swerve from
his position. He saw clearly what needed to be said and
he said it: any idea is true insofar as it works and any
idea that works is insofar true. The added "insofar"
seemed to many to be a weasel word which did not contribute much to the discussion. James, on the other hand,
saw it as adding precision to the definition and in fact it
did. To realize this, however, it was necessary to take
seriously the pragmatic theory of meaning and its principle that the meaning of an idea consists in its practical
consequences. Consider, for example, the idea in the thirteenth century that the earth was flat. One of the practical
consequences of this idea would be that if you were plot-
ting a course for a vessel to cross the English Channel
you would plot a Euclidean straight line. This statement
was true then and it is true now. So-called great-circle
navigation which is used to plot the shortest route on the
earth's surface, produces a straight line for such short
distances. What this amounts to is that, when taken in
small segments, the surface of the earth is indistinguish-
able from a flat surface. Therefore *insofar as* the statement "the earth is flat" meant "when traveling short distances on the earth's surface follow a Euclidean straight
line," this statement was true—and is still true. Thus
if we listed a total of twenty practical consequences that
followed from the theory and found that seven of them
worked in the thirteenth century, they would still work
today. And the statement "the earth is flat" would be true
insofar as it meant those seven consequences. Ergo, an
idea is true insofar as it works.

The true, to put it very briefly, is only the expedient in the way of thinking. . . . Expedient in almost any fashion; and expedient in the long run and on the whole of course; for what meets expediently all the experience in sight won't necessarily meet all farther experiences equally satisfactorily. . . . Meanwhile we have to live today by what truth we can get today, and be ready tomorrow to call it falsehood. Ptolemaic astronomy, euclidean space, aristotelian logic, scholastic metaphysics, were expedient for centuries, but human experience has boiled over those limits, and we now call these things only relatively true, or true within the borders of experience. "Absolutely" they are false; for we know that those limits were casual, and might have been transcended by past theorists just as they are by present thinkers.[15]

Another aspect of the problem was not dealt with very successfully by James. This was the matter of the meaning of truth with reference to so-called historical propositions or propositions about the past. Is it true to say that "Julius Caesar crossed the Rubicon"? An appropriate answer would be: "It is true if Caesar crossed the Rubicon." But the problem is: how do we know whether Caesar did this? We cannot go back in time and watch Caesar and see whether he was able to cross the Rubicon. If true ideas are those we can verify, how can we verify propositions about the past? On this point James says:

The overwhelming majority of our true ideas admit of no direct or face-to-face verification—those of past history, for example, as of Cain and Abel. The stream of time can be remounted only verbally, or verified indirectly by the present prolongations or effects of what the past harbored. Yet if they agree with these verbalities and effects, we can know that our ideas of the past are true. *As true as past time itself was,* so true was Julius Caesar, so true were antediluvian monsters, all in their proper dates and settings. That past time itself was, is guaranteed by its coherence with everything that's present. True as the present *is,* the past *was* also.[16]

This is nice rhetoric, but we expect something better from a pragmatist. We cannot verify Caesar's existence directly, nor can we verify it "indirectly." While it is true that we have, for example, books purportedly written by Julius Caesar, *that* they were in fact written by Caesar is in no way a verifiable proposition. So that the "indirect" proofs are as unverifiable as the direct proofs.

James comes closer to the target when he says: "That past time itself was, is guaranteed by its coherence with everything that's present." If we take this to mean not anything about past time, but rather something about our "idea of past time," and, specifically, to mean that that idea works in explaining things presently in the world, such a statement would be reasonably correct. We could thus say that our "idea of past time" was true.

Since, in the pragmatic view, every idea is a statement about experiences we may expect and reactions we will prepare—i.e., every idea is a series of predictions about future experiences—we must conclude that our idea of the past is essentially a series of predictions about the future. If these predictions turn out to work, then our idea about the past was true. This paradoxical twist was described by George Santayana as "the pragmatic reduction of yesterday to tomorrow."

That our ideas of the past are essentially references

to the future may be illustrated by borrowing from an example of Bertrand Russell's. Russell suggested that if the world had been created only five minutes ago—so that there was no past—with everything exactly as it now is, each of us with his present memories, etc., none of us would know the difference. This would seem to be correct. In such a situation, if someone doubted that Christopher Columbus ever really existed, we would take him to the libraries and museums and show him the same books and charts we would now show him. The "proofs" that Columbus lived are the same whether he lived or not, and that is because these "proofs" are statements about the future, i.e., about what we *would* find if we went to the libraries, the museums, etc.

A final element that needs to be discussed in James's analysis of truth is the extent to which he understood truth to be a function of human beliefs and desires. Ordinarily we tend to feel that our ideas and beliefs should be determined by the objects in the external world, the "facts." To hold to the reverse of this—that what the external world is will be determined by what we may think about it—sounds almost like lunacy. In addition to holding that what we believed about the world was an important element in determining what the truth about the world was ("the world stands really malleable, waiting to receive its final touches at our hands . . . man engenders truth upon it"),[17] James held further that our desires also determined what was true. "The true is the name of whatever proves itself to be good in the way of belief, and good, too, for definite assignable reasons. . . . Ought we ever not to believe what it is *better for us* to believe?"[18] "If theological ideas prove to have a value for concrete life, they will be true, for pragmatism, in the sense of being good for so much."[19]

With James talking in this way, it is no great surprise

that he found his critics to be describing his view as that of someone who holds that "by saying whatever you find it pleasant to say and calling it truth you fulfill every pragmatistic requirement."[20]

A complete exposition of why James held this view can only come after we have examined his metaphysics in later chapters, but a few points can be made now. A major element in James's thinking on the nature of truth was his conviction of the extent to which "truth" in science is more a function of the observer than of that which is observed. We have referred to this above. James restates it when he says in the book *The Meaning of Truth*:

As I understand the pragmatist way of seeing things, it owes its being to the breakdown which the last fifty years have brought about in the older notion of scientific truth. "God geometrizes," it used to be said; and it was believed that Euclid's elements literally reproduced his geometrizing. There is an eternal and unchangeable "reason"; and its voice was supposed to reverberate in *Barbara* and *Celarent*. So also of the "laws of nature," physical and chemical, so of natural history classifications—all were supposed to be exact and exclusive duplicates of pre-human archetypes buried in the structure of things, to which the spark of divinity hidden in our intellect enables us to penetrate. The anatomy of the world is logical, and its logic is that of a university professor, it was thought. Up to about 1850 almost everyone believed that sciences expressed truths that were exact copies of a definite code of non-human realities. But the enormously rapid multiplication of theories in these latter days has well-nigh upset the notion of any one of them being a more literally objective kind of thing than another. There are so many geometrics, so many logics, so many physical and chemical hypotheses, so many classifications, each one of them good for so much and yet not good for everything, that the notion that even the truest formula may be a human device and not a literal transcript has dawned upon us. . . . It is to be doubted whether any theorizer today, either in mathematics, logic, physics or biology, conceives himself to be literally re-editing processes of nature or thoughts of God.[21]

The other way in which man's desires affected truth lay in what James made a basic component of his philosophy. James, more genuinely than any of his critics seem to have realized, simply believed in an open universe. The destiny of the universe was not predetermined from all eternity. Its end was not settled by the first day of creation. Even God could not know how it would come out. The end was genuinely indetermined. In such an open-ended universe, the materials are given, but many alternatives are possible using the same materials. "We receive in short the block of marble, but we carve the statue ourselves."[22]

In this process of "making a universe" James thoroughly believed in the efficacy of the human contribution to the ultimate resolution of the indeterminacy. "We have only one edition of the universe, unfinished, growing in all sorts of places, especially in the places where thinking beings are at work."[23] This notion that human beings were not just puppets of the gods, playing out a role in some drama they never wrote and whose end was settled beyond any of their doing, was one of the points of contact between the view of James and that of F. C. S. Schiller, the British philosopher who became associated with the American movement of pragmatism. Borrowing Schiller's name for this belief that human beings could affect the world by their desires, James called it humanism. It was a major element in his reaction against the Calvinistic doctrine of the impotence of man in the face of the omnipotence of God. It meant that human beings did count for something in the long sweep of history. James says: "No one can deny that such a role would add both to our dignity and to our responsibility as thinkers."[24] We return to this point in a later chapter.

If instead of emphasizing the aspect of humanism that stressed the increase in human dignity, one stressed the fact that man could act and by acting affect his destiny, one got the more "activist" pragmatism of the young Italian, Papini, whose work seems to have had some effect on Mussolini.

This notion allows for some leeway in our beliefs. We may believe what is better for us to believe, because by so believing we may help to make truth. But this does not mean we are free to believe anything whatever. There is a narrow segment of beliefs which are held in areas where genuine alternatives are still open because neither established theory nor ascertained fact has spoken to decide the issue. Again the process is illustrated by reference to science:

> In the choice of these man-made formulas we can not be capricious with impunity any more than we can be capricious on the common-sense level. We must find a theory that will *work;* and that means something extremely difficult; for our theory must mediate between all previous truths and certain new experiences. It must derange common sense and previous belief as little as possible, and it must lead to some sensible terminus or other that can be veri-

fied exactly. To "work" means both these things; and the squeeze is so tight that there is little loose play for any hypothesis. Our theories are wedged and controlled as nothing else is. Yet sometimes alternative theoretic formulas are equally compatible with all the truths we know, and then we choose between them for subjective reasons. We choose the kind of theory to which we are already partial; we follow "elegance" or "economy. . . ." Truth in science is what gives the maximum possible sum of satisfactions, taste included, but consistency both with previous truth and with novel fact is always the most imperious claimant.[25]

James found among his critics many persons who felt that since the word "truth" was a noun, there must somehow be something which this noun named. James saw that this was not the case. Many of the apparent paradoxes in his theory of truth flow from this conviction. He was fond of quoting Lord Salisbury's remark that the word "ether" was simply the noun form of the verb "to undulate." Similarly, James thought, the word "truth" was simply the noun form of the verb "to verify." In describing the pragmatist's position, he said: "Truth for us is simply a collective name for verification processes . . ."[26] He pointed out that many words in English ending in *th* had this characteristic of naming processes, not things. "Health, wealth, strength, etc. are names for other processes connected with life . . ."[27] Suppose you were trying to teach someone what health was, and when you pointed to a healthy man your student said: "No, I don't want to see an example of health, I want to see health itself." You would probably reply: "Health is a process exhibited by living organisms when they behave in a certain way; it is not a thing which exists by itself. It is a collective name for certain life processes." Similar arguments would apply for wealth and strength.

If we think of truth in this way, if we mean by it certain life processes, then the pragmatic paradox does indeed follow that: "Truth is *made,* just as health, wealth and strength are made, in the course of experience."[28]

Our language usage recognizes wealth as something that is "made." Strength and health are also made, as when we "rebuild" them after a long illness. If truth is a name for the biological processes of verifying our ideas, then it would follow not only that truth is made, but also the further pragmatic paradox that truth—like health, wealth, and strength—*grows.*

Among the processes that human beings engage in there will be some that make us feel vigorous and happy. These processes that make us feel "whole" came to get a class name "wholth," which eventually became health. Other processes are of use in earning money, others in building muscles. We mark out of the chaos of processes certain ones which have common characteristics and we give this subclass of processes a name for purposes of reference. We are particularly apt to do this if the subclass appeals to us or is of value to us.

Upon seeking to classify and order this chaos of processes so that we can think about it and understand it, we look for these subgroups and organize our biological behaviors into them wherever we can. One such subgroup that comes early to our notice is that of the processes which work successfully. The ones that do what we want them to do. The ones which pay. The ones which it is expedient to follow. Thus we get the pragmatist paradox that truths are those processes which "it pays to pursue."[29] "The true . . . is only the expedient in our way of thinking."[30]

The specific behavior patterns which will be included in

the subclass truth—i.e., the ideas we will call true—will accordingly vary from one period in history to another. With increasing knowledge and increasing social complexity, behavior patterns which worked at one time will not work at another, and so what ideas are true will indeed be different at one time as against another. Eventually from this sifting and sorting we may reach a group of behavior processes which are such that they will work in all further experience. If so, we will have absolute truths. At this point, once again, there will be many persons who will wish to part company with James.

> The "absolutely" true, meaning what no farther experience will ever alter, is that ideal vanishing-point toward which we imagine that all our temporary truths will some day converge. . . . Like the half-truths, the absolute truth will have to be *made,* made as a relation incidental to the growth of a mass of verification-experiences, to which the half-true ideas are all along contributing their quota.[31]

It is possible to understand James's philosophy most adequately if we constantly keep in mind that he came into philosophy by way of psychology and into psychology by way of physiology and medicine. John Locke was one of James's favorite philosophers. Locke was also a physician who became fascinated with epistemology. James likes to feel that he is following Locke in his insistence upon thought processes as beginning and ending in physiological sensations or behaviors. James stood in many ways where the modern behavioral psychologist stands. We shall see this again in the next chapter. It may be seen in the present context by the following summary of his view of truth.

Essentially, as we have seen, James's pragmatic theory

of truth was a version of the correspondence theory of truth. He readily admitted that for an idea to be true it must correspond with reality. However, his most fundamental insight—which his critics did not readily see—was that correspondence was a function of the idea, not of the reality. The reality had to be there for the idea to be true. But the reality was there in exactly the same way if the idea was false. It followed that the difference between truth and falsity must be due to something in the idea, not in the reality.*

If we ask what it means practically for an idea to "correspond" with a reality, we see that it means something about our behavior. It means that when we behave toward the object in those ways which the idea prescribes, our behavior works successfully in enabling us to deal with the object. This behavior—and its success or lack of it—was a public and observable thing. So that truth was not a private, subjective property possessed only by the individual on the basis of a private intuition. It was a publicly observable and publicly testable property of an idea. A man's behavior showed whether his ideas were true. By prescribing the appropriate behaviors for other observers, they too could verify his ideas.

There were two matters which kept clouding James's discussion of truth, so that his critics often had difficulty seeing what he was saying. They felt either that he was not paying sufficient attention to older, established truths, or that he allowed truth to be settled by resort to emotion. These two red herrings got regularly dragged across the trail of the polemic between James and his critics.

Among James's critics it was generally the coherence-

---

* "The difference is that when the pragmatists speak of truth, they mean exclusively something about the idea . . . whereas when anti-pragmatists speak of truth they seem most often to mean something about the objects."[32]

theory group—who considered an idea to be true if it cohered with other ideas—who felt that James paid insufficient attention to already known truths. James undertook to reply on many occasions that this was an important aspect of the matter. Other things being equal, we would accept the idea that disrupted our already existing body of beliefs with the least friction. But, for James, this could not be the basic criterion of truth. This criterion would bar us from accepting the occasional truth that completely disrupted former beliefs. Darwin's theory of evolution and the discovery of radioactive elements which seemed to be creating energy out of nothing were examples of such new truths. In these cases we would seek for an explanation which disturbed our former beliefs as little as possible, but we could not reject evolution or radioactivity simply because they did not agree with our previous beliefs. This would be saying that correspondence with the past was the main criterion of truth. What James's pragmatism required him to look for was correspondence with the future—predictions of sense experiences and actions.

The other red herring was the way in which emotional attitudes entered into the truth process. This difficulty came from James rather than from his opponents. James asked: what do we do when we have two beliefs which appear to account equally well for all the known data—Ptolemy versus Copernicus, God versus no-god, free will versus determinism? The traditional answer as to the proper decision procedure, when faced with two equally good theories, was either to remain in a state of suspended belief—agnosticism in religion, for example—or to choose the theory which was simpler (Occam's razor), as in preferring Copernicus to Ptolemy.

James rejected the notion of agnosticism in the decision-making process because he was convinced that human behavior was efficacious in deciding many issues. Accordingly the human being who refused to act in favor of a theory (the agnostic), by his very inaction might render that theory incapable of realization. Accordingly, said James, when we have two equally plausible theories we ought to select the one we would like to see realized and work for it. Thus if, but only if, sense experience and reason could not decide between theories, emotion was a suitable arbitrator.

To this the reply could be made that science already had a technique for deciding between alternatively adequate theories, namely Occam's razor—do not multiply entities unnecessarily—which was interpreted to mean that we should always select the simpler of two alternative theories rather than selecting the one we would like to see true. But if we ask ourselves what is meant by "simpler" in this context, the notion that Occam's razor renders a rational decision untouched by emotion does not seem so obvious. The unsophisticated reader often thinks "simplicity" is established by some such process as counting the number of cycles and epicycles in Ptolemy's theory and finding that this number exceeds the number of orbits in the theory of Copernicus. In fact, however, what is usually meant by "simplicity" in a theory approaches more precisely to what the mathematicians call "elegance." Thus if the wave-particle duality in physics is resolved by the development of a unitary "waveicle" theory, the latter theory may have a mathematical and experimental structure of much greater complexity than its two predecessors combined, but it will be preferred because it will be "simpler." If the effort to combine gravitational-field equations with electromagnetic-field equations should succeed, such a "unified field theory" will be simpler even though its mathematics may require the invention of a new kind of calculus or geometry. "Simplicity" or "elegance" is not a property of the mathematics but of the mathematician. What scientists really find is that they "like" one kind of theory better than another—that is, it is aesthetically more appealing. Now, unless we wish to hold that a scientist's choice between theories is not based on emotion but rather upon an "instinct" for correct theories (as Charles Peirce did, and in contemporary literature see Michael Polanyi's *Personal Knowledge*[33]), then we must hold that the scientist's picking of the theory he "likes" is no more valid than anyone else picking—between alternates which account equally well for the facts—a different theory for different emotional reasons. When it comes to choosing between "likings," one "liking" is as good as another.

The only way in which James ever wished to allow a "liking" or "satisfying" to determine truth was where the alternates accounted equally well for the facts and our efforts might influence the result. Under these circumstances, if we had a strong emotional preference for one theory rather than another, our right to choose the one we liked was as valid as was the scientist's right to choose the one he liked.

Chapter 4

METAPHYSICS:
EMPIRICISM AND PLURALISM

In 1885 James wrote a penetrating essay titled "The Function of Cognition." He reprinted the essay, virtually unchanged, as the opening paper of his book *The Meaning of Truth* in 1909. The essay is intrinsically interesting, but historically it is worth noting that it asserts most of the fundamental doctrines of James's philosophy as he was to argue them for the next twenty-five years. Significant differences between this early statement and the later doctrines of pragmatism, truth, and pure experience are hard to find.

The term "cognition" in this essay means knowledge. Specifically it means knowledge descriptive of a reality. Such knowledge is an idea or a thought or a "feeling"—this latter term being used by James as a synonym for any state of consciousness.[1] In the cognitive process there will be at least three fundamental items: the idea, the external reality, and a relation between them. If the idea is to know anything more than itself it must somehow transcend itself and, by means of the relation, get to the reality. If, upon doing so, it finds the reality to be "like" itself in some way, it is said to be an idea about the reality—to resemble the reality. Accordingly we have a number of questions: What is an idea? What is a reality? How do we know when they "resemble" one another?

In discussing the nature of an idea James makes a well-known distinction between "knowledge by acquaintance" (knowledge of) and "knowledge about" (knowledge by description). The former of these is essentially a percept or sense experience, a visual, auditory, or tactual image, for example. We are acquainted with a thing when we know it directly in the intimate fashion that gives us sense experiences of it. Knowledge about, on the other hand, is conceptual knowledge. We have a concept rather than a percept. Our knowledge is of the intellect rather than of the senses.

If cognition is merely knowledge by acquaintance, if it is only sensory images, if these images are not interpreted by a concept, then the images are meaningless. They are like a motion picture being shown in an empty theater. To try to get anything from them alone is, says James, "milking a he-goat." For the sense experiences to "mean" anything they must be interpreted by a concept which categorizes them and speaks to their significance. Without concepts, percepts are dumb.

On the other hand, what about concepts without percepts? Suppose we have only knowledge "about" a thing but no knowledge "of" it. Our knowledge is of a meager and unsatisfactory kind. We are like a person who has been told about something he has never seen. We cannot "know" what a toothache is if we have never had one.

There were prominent philosophers in James's day—the group he called the intellectualists—who derided perceptual knowledge as vague, inaccurate, and unreliable. They preferred to preserve the honorific term "knowledge" only for rational concepts. James, on the contrary, thought that concepts come from percepts. Let the idea "be fragrance, let it be a toothache, or let it be a more complex kind of feeling, like that of the full moon swimming in her blue abyss, it must first come in that simple shape . . . before any knowledge *about* it can be attained."[2]

The concept, then, is *about* something. It is *about* percepts. This gives us an initial orientation toward a pragmatic theory of meaning: what percepts (sense experiences and reactions) is the concept about, what percept does it refer to, intend, denote, mean, or signify?

Before answering that question we may want to look at a prior question. If concepts are about percepts, what are percepts about? What do they point to? The usual answer is a reality. But how do we know that? How can we tell that percepts transcend themselves and somehow point to a reality? Suppose all realities were gone, but the percepts remained? Would we know the difference? We have thus the problem posed by the subjective idealists since the time of George Berkeley. The uninitiated in philosophy is apt to think that he would know by means of his percepts if the reality were not there. What Berkeley pointed out was that all our knowledge was in fact limited to percepts. If there is a reality beyond the percepts we never know *it*, but only our sense experiences of it. Thus a person who eats a fish "knows" he is doing so because he has a visual percept of a fish, plus a fish taste and a fish smell, followed by a sense of having had something to eat, followed in turn by the ensuing sense of physical growth and development of his body. But suppose all these sense experiences to be present and no fish really to be there? Would we know the difference? Clearly not, as Berkeley points out. What we know are our sense experiences, not the reality. Just as a person in a dream believes the reality to be there—otherwise a nightmare would not have the power to frighten—so we may simply be the recipients of an orderly sequence of sense experiences (coming from God, in Berkeley's view) without ever actually having any real objects externally present to produce these ideas.

This view—that all that exists is our ideas—is known in epistemology as idealism. Its opposite—the belief in real external objects—is known as realism. James was committed to realism. For a realist the problem is how to bridge the "epistemological gulf" and get to the real object, how to know that it is there.

This is a problem no epistemologist has ever solved. The only way we get to know realities is through sense experiences of them. But to know that the reality exists independently of our sense experiences, we would have to "know" it at a time when we were not having a sense experience of it—when we were not seeing it, touching it, or hearing it, for instance. But this kind of knowledge is manifestly impossible, at least for the empiricist. Unless we wish to admit—as James did not—some "higher" form of knowledge— such as intuition or reason—which can know without seeing, hearing, touching, etc., then we can only say that knowledge of a reality outside of sense knowledge is impossible.

This problem in epistemology was later identified and named by James's student Ralph Barton Perry as "the ego-centric predicament." We are in the predicament that all knowledge that we know, *we* know. So that we cannot know how things are "independently of a knower." We are like the small boy who wanted to see whether the room was any different when no one was looking at it and so went outside and took a quick look in through a window to see how the room looked when it was not being looked at.

There is no way to solve this awkward problem. We cannot "prove" the external reality to really be there independently of our sensing of it. There are three traditional paths to follow at this point. One is that of the idealist: to say that we ought not to believe in what we cannot prove and to deny the existence of "real" objects. A second is that of the positivist: to say that we can neither believe nor disbelieve because we know nothing about "external" objects—the term cannot convey any knowledge to be believed or disbelieved and so is meaningless. The third path is that of the realist, whose sense of reality is too robust for these alternatives and who must, therefore, believe in the existence of realities without direct evidence. James is a realist in this latter sense.

> . . . What becomes our warrant for calling anything reality? The only reply is—the faith of the present critic or inquirer. At every moment of his life he finds himself subject to a belief in *some* realities, even though his realities of this year should prove to be his illusions of the next.[3]

This assumption—that we can somehow know external realities—is a necessary assumption for a realist in epistemology, but it is also the source of error when we overshoot the evidence and believe in realities beyond the limits of the evidence.

> Every science must make some assumptions. *Erkenntnisstheoretiker* are but fallible mortals. When they study the function of cognition, they do it by means of the same function in themselves. And knowing that the fountain cannot go higher than its source, we should promptly confess that our results in this field are affected by our liability to err.[4]

James wished to be considered a realist. In 1909 he wrote of this early article that in it "we find distinctly asserted:—1. The reality, external to the true idea . . ."⁵ However, he also says in this article that "These percepts, these *termini,* these sensible things, these mere matters-of-acquaintance, are the only realities we ever directly know, and the whole history of our thought is the history of our substitution of one of them for another, and the reduction of the substitute to the status of a conceptual sign."⁶

If all we ever know are the percepts, what warrant is there for a belief in unknown "external realities"? James's answer is: they act upon us (they produce percepts) and we act upon them (producing changes in our percepts). Thus the production of percepts in us and the consequent production of actions altering these percepts are the characteristic processes by which we are most intimately in touch with reality. This indirect knowledge of realities is all we have. It is a knowledge that begins in percepts and moves through action to conclude in percepts. This analysis of the knowledge process leads inevitably to a pragmatic criterion of knowledge and meaning. James concludes the article by saying:

Contemned though they be by some thinkers, these sensations are the mother-earth, the anchorage, the stable rock, the first and last limits, the *terminus a quo* and the *terminus ad quem* of the mind. To find such sensational *termini* should be our aim with all our higher thought. They end discussion; they destroy the false conceit of knowledge; and without them we are all at sea with each other's meanings. If two men act alike on a percept, they believe themselves to feel alike about it; if not, they may suspect they know it in different ways. We can never be sure we understand each other till we are able to bring the matter to this test. This is why metaphysical discussions are so much like fighting with the air; they have no practical issue of a sensational kind. "Scientific" theories, on the other hand, always terminate in definite percepts. You can deduce a possible sensation from your theory and, taking me into your laboratory, prove that your theory is true of my world by giving me the sensation then and there.[7]

This is a perfectly precise statement of the pragmatic doctrine in this 1885 article—long before the 1898 article that started the pragmatic movement. That James was this early influenced by Charles Peirce is seen in his footnote to the above paragraph, in which he quotes the pragmatic maxim from Peirce's 1878 article:

"There is no distinction of meaning so fine as to consist in anything but a possible difference of practice. . . . It appears, then, that the rule for attaining the [highest] grade of clearness of apprehension is as follows: Consider what effects, which might conceivably have practical bearings, we conceive the object of our conception to have. Then, our conception of these effects is the whole of our conception of the object." Charles S. Peirce: "How to make our ideas clear," in *Popular Science Monthly,* New York, January, 1878, p. 293.

At this point we may examine a question that is fundamental: How do we know when an idea or a percept "refers to" or knows something else? This notion of "referring to" is crucial both to James's theory of pragmatism and to his pragmatic theory of truth. The theory of pragmatism says that two apparently different ideas are the same if they refer to the same percepts. But how do we know what percepts they refer to? James's theory of truth requires that an idea is true if it "refers to" a reality. But how, again, do we establish reference?

What we need is a criterion of "reference." Under what circumstances will we say that reference prevails and under what circumstances will we say that it is absent?

In seeking to answer this question, James points out that "resemblance" is not enough to constitute reference. An idea does not necessarily know an object simply because it "resembles" it. "Eggs resemble each other, but do not on that account represent, stand for, or know each other."[8] For an idea to know an object it must not only resemble the object but point to the object, refer to it as the object it resembles. So our problem becomes one of determining when an idea knows an object, as ascertained by determining what object it is pointing to or referring to.

James uses the analogy of a gun. The gun shows which reality it is pointing to "by *breaking* it."[9] The gun does something to the reality, it affects it, it operates on it. Can we establish a parallel definition for an idea? Are there operational effects of an idea that mark out as flagrantly the reality the idea refers to? James thinks there are. If the idea is *of* a reality, then the idea has effects; it operates on the reality. This operation in turn produces as a consequence some change in my percepts. Thus we get an operational definition of "referring to" which says that an idea "refers to" a reality when action on the basis of the idea produces consequences which effect a change in my percepts of the reality. These "practical consequences" come to be the criterion of what is meant by "referring to." Does my idea of that apple refer to that apple? I act on the idea; I pick the apple up and take a bite. My percept of the apple is altered. I thus know that it was indeed "that apple" that my idea referred to.

This operational definition of "knowing" is expressed by James thus: "A percept knows whatever reality it directly or indirectly operates on and resembles; a conceptual feeling, or thought knows a reality, whenever it actually or potentially terminates in a percept that operates on, or resembles that reality, or is otherwise connected with it or with its context."[10]

This definition has quite a contemporary ring to it. James realized that it did not solve all of the problems involved. The definition does not guarantee that we have been in contact with a reality. It says that when we act in accord with our idea of a reality and find that we have an expected change in our percepts, we may then say, by definition, that we have been in contact with the reality. But we must assume the existence of the reality, as we have seen earlier; we cannot experience it directly. From the behavior of our percepts—which we do experience directly—we infer the existence of a reality which we do not experience except indirectly through the percepts.

Similarly with the problem of a common world. You have your percepts and I have mine. How do I know yours refer to the same world as mine?

In the last analysis, then, we believe that we all know and think about and talk about the same world because *we believe our PERCEPTS are possessed by us in common*. And we believe this because the percepts of each one of us seem to be changed in consequence of changes in the percepts of someone else.[11]

[123]

So the problems of the existence of an external world and of other minds are resolved by James by definition. He fails to establish that they exist. Here he shares a failure that extends to all forms of empiricism. That an external world exists, that other minds exist, ". . . is something of which we never can be sure, but which we assume as the simplest hypothesis that meets the case."[12]

Thus James makes his basic epistemological assumptions: there are external objects and knowing minds. The circumstances under which they are defined as interacting are given by the operational definition which is expressed summarily by him as the view that an idea *"knows whatever reality it resembles, and either directly or indirectly operates on.* If it resembles without operating, it is a dream; if it operates without resembling, it is an error."[13]

From this general epistemological position stated in 1885, James was to proceed to a full version of his "radical empiricism" in his later writings between 1900 and his death. In these writings the external objects and other minds are removed from the realm of the "unknowable" and brought into the realm of that which can be known.

In dealing with the problem of bridging the gap between the idea and the object, James's first effort lay in arguing that the gap—the "epistemological chasm'" as he called it—was an invention of his opponents. He distinguished between what he called the "saltatory" and the "ambulatory" views of the knowledge process. The traditional epistemology saw the knowing mind as separated from the known object by the epistemological gulf, so that the only way for knowledge to get from the object to the mind was for either the mind or the object to somehow jump this gulf (take it by assault—hence "saltatory"). The alternative view provided intermediate points by which the mind moved closer step by step (to ambulate—hence "ambulatory").

> Cognition, whenever we take it concretely, means determinate "ambulation," through intermediaries, from a *terminus a quo* to, or towards, a *terminus ad quem*. . . . But there exist no processes which we cannot also consider abstractly, eviscerating them down to their essential skeletons or outlines; and when we have treated the processes of knowing thus, we are easily led to regard them as something altogether unparalleled in nature. . . . In other words, the intermediaries which in their concrete particularity form a bridge, evaporate ideally into an empty interval to cross, and then, the relation of the endterms having become saltatory, the whole hocuspocus of *erkenntnisstheorie* begins and goes on unrestrained by further concrete considerations.[14]

The intermediaries to which James was here referring were sense experiences or percepts. I have a certain idea of an object. This idea has certain practical consequences of an experiential sort. For example, I see something I have never seen before. Since I see it I have the idea it can be touched, so I reach out to touch it. I get a cool, hard percept. I have taken the first step toward getting knowledge of the object. I lift it; I have a percept of heaviness. I put my tongue to it and get a metallic taste. I take it to the laboratory and perform a chemical analysis of part of it. I examine it microscopically to see if it is alive. I seek to determine the conditions under which it will grow and to ascertain uses to which it may be put. With each of these added percepts of the object, my "knowing" of it is increased and my knowledge added to. Each such experience is a further step toward "knowing" the object. Such steps do not take place outside of experience in some mysterious epistemological process, but go on wholly within the context of my experience. Knowing is not a mysterious process, but a natural one.

Knowledge of sensible realities thus comes to life inside the tissue of experience. It is *made;* and made by relations that unroll themselves in time. Whenever certain intermediaries are given such that as they develop towards their terminus, there is experience from point to point of one direction followed, and finally of one process fulfilled, the result is that *their starting-point thereby becomes a knower and their terminus an object meant or known.*[15]

The effect of such a description of the knowledge process is to give us no absolute knowledge. Knowledge of an object changes as new experiences are had of it. If we ever got to a point where all possible experiences had been had, then we would have absolute knowledge. But since we would not know that no further new experiences were possible, we would not know that we had absolute knowledge.

Our whole notion of a standing reality grows up in the form of an ideal limit to the series of successive termini to which our thoughts have led and still are leading us. Each terminus proves provisional by leaving us unsatisfied. The truer idea is the one that pushes farther; so we are ever beckoned on by the ideal notion of an ultimate completely satisfactory terminus.[16]

Finally, when we say an idea is true we mean to say that the idea when acted upon does lead us up to the object more closely than any other idea we know. So that this leading satisfactorily through a series of sensible experiences up to a predicted set of percepts turns out to be the process of verifying an idea or establishing its truth.

Each reality verifies and validates its own idea exclusively; and in each case the verification consists in the satisfactorily-ending consequences, mental or physical, which the idea was able to set up. These "workings" differ in every single instance, they never transcend experience, they consist of particulars, mental or sensible, and they admit of concrete description in every individual case.[17]

It is evident that James liked to think of himself as a realist for whom an independent external world really existed, and felt that he was justified in inferring that there were external objects.[18] However, this inference does not give him any warrant beyond that of plausibility. We never experience the external object. We only "experience our experiences" of it. James's external object is remarkably analogous to John Locke's "unknown somewhat." We know nothing about it except that it is. Under these circumstances it becomes difficult to say much about the object. All we really need to do is talk about our experiences.

A second problem in this same connection arose from the mind-body problem. How can an idea, which is a mental thing, "know" an object which is a physical thing? It may perhaps approximate knowledge of it, the way a citizen of the United States may know approximately what it is like to be a citizen of China or India. But can we ever "know" these things completely and absolutely? Can a man ever know what it is like to be a tree? Or a chair? Or a bird? Our ambulatory experiences may bring us closer and closer to these things, but can they ever bring us right up to them so we identify with them and know them completely? It would seem not; as long as they are physical things and our ideas are mental images of them, the image can never "be" the thing in the way in which complete knowledge would appear to require.

Ether-waves and your anger, for example, are things in which my thoughts will never *perceptually* terminate, but my concepts of them lead me to their very brink, to the chromatic fringes and to the hurtful words and deeds which are their really next effects.[19]

But coming to the brink and fringes of objects is not full knowledge of them. And if this is the best we can do, a full knowledge would seem to be impossible. In fact it would seem to be difficult to find any warrant for even calling our partial or approximate knowledge, knowledge of the objects. It is only knowledge of our percepts.

James is forced to talk in a very strange way to avoid these difficulties. Thus he wrote in 1904 that by reality he meant "nothing more than the other conceptual or perceptual experiences with which a given present experience may find itself in point of fact mixed up."[20] To say that one means by reality "nothing more than other experiences" certainly sounds like idealism. However, to this statement James adds a footnote asserting that he is a realist: "This is meant merely to exclude reality of an 'unknowable' sort, of which no account in either perceptual or conceptual terms can be given. It includes of course any amount of empirical reality independent of the knower. Pragmatism is thus 'epistemologically' realistic in its accounts."[21]

To reconcile these apparently conflicting statements James needed to become a metaphysical (ontological) idealist and an epistemological realist. That is, he had to assert that the fundamental nature of things was somehow or other of the nature of an idea, while at the same time such ideas had a reality independent of the knowing mind.

This difficulty should have led James—as it did others of his contemporaries, e.g., Josiah Royce and Charles S. Peirce—to a form of objective idealism. He should have held that there were real objects independent of the knower but that these objects were mental in nature.

James sought, very ingeniously, to undercut this problem. The traditional choices open to a philosopher would allow for the following alternatives in metaphysics: (1) Metaphysical dualism: the assertion that both mind and matter existed. The difficulty here was that of the mind-body problem. (2) Metaphysical monism: the assertion that either mind was basic (idealism) and matter an unwarranted inference, or that matter was basic (materialism) and mind was simply a function of matter. James wanted to have it both ways. He wanted to say that matter did not exist as an independent entity and thus avoid the difficulties of the mind-body problem, and he wanted to say that mind did not exist as an independent entity but only as a function.[22] Now, this approach itself posed some difficulties. If both matter and mind were eliminated, what was left?

What James did was to postulate a new basic substance which was neither mind nor matter. It could, under appropriate circumstances, become either, but it was "neutral" in respect to the mind-matter decision. Since there was to be only one such substance, the view was a metaphysical monism, but since the substance was neutral on the mind-matter issue, it was a "neutral" monism.

This development of the theory of a substance prior

to mind or matter of which they were only aspects was an original contribution by James to the problem. There were some similarities to it in Spinoza and Leibniz but their contexts were clearly different. The theory has had few adherents since James—although Bertrand Russell at one point in his career held a quite similar view.

James seems to have come to his view from his efforts as a psychologist and an epistemologist to attain a satisfactory description of the process of cognition and of the operation of consciousness. As early as 1895, in his presidential address before the American Psychological Association, he was saying of the process of knowing a piece of white paper that "the paper seen and the seeing of it are only two names for one indivisible fact which, properly named, is *the datum, the phenomenon, or the experience.* The paper is in the mind and the mind is around the paper, because paper and mind are only two names that are given later to the one experience, when, taken in a larger world of which it forms a part, its connections are traced in different directions."[23]

What James is developing during these years is the notion that there is a basic stuff that is neutral as to its being mental or physical. If it is taken in one context— "your experiences"—it is a mental experience; if it is taken in another context it is a physical thing's experience. But in itself it is neither a mental experience nor a physical experience. It is a "pure" experience. James's doctrine of pure experience may be illustrated by the analogy of a road intersection.[24] If an accident occurs at the intersection of Main Street and Jones Avenue, an observer standing down the block on Main Street and looking at the accident will see it as an event on Main Street. An observer standing down the block on Jones Avenue and looking at the event will see it as an event on Jones Avenue. Whether the accident is a "Main

Street event" or a "Jones Avenue event" depends upon the context in which we take it. So with a pure experience. Taken in one context it is a mental experience, taken in another context it is a physical experience. Whether an event is a mind event or a matter event depends upon the context in which we take it.

Thus I am writing this at a wooden desk. As I look at the desk it becomes a part of my experiences. Just before I looked at the desk I was talking to my young son. Shortly I will eat lunch. Taken in this sequence of events, the wooden desk is a mental thing in my chain of experiences proceeding from "talking to son," "looking at desk," "eating lunch." But taken in another way, the desk is an event in the life history of a piece of wood. The wood grew somewhere in a forest, was cut down, made into a desk, sold to me, is now being looked at by me, will someday be destroyed by fire or decay. Considered from this point of view, my writing on the desk and looking at it are events in the desk's history as a physical object.

Accordingly we may conclude that the desk is a mental thing when taken in the context of my experiences or a physical thing when taken in the context of the world's experiences. Basically the desk is neither a mental experience nor a physical experience; it is a pure experience that may be taken either way.

In his essay "Does 'Consciousness' Exist?" in 1904, James wrote:

> My thesis is that if we start with the supposition that there is only one primal stuff or material in the world, a stuff of which everything is composed, and if we call that stuff "pure experience," then knowing can easily be explained as a particular sort of rela-

tion towards one another into which portions of pure experience may enter. The relation itself is a part of pure experience, one of its "terms" becomes the subject or bearer of the knowledge, the knower, the other becomes the object known.[25]

James denies that experience shows the "duplicity" of mental idea and physical object. The duplicity is only the same thing taken in two contexts. He uses the illustration of paint:

In a pot in a paint-shop, along with other paints, it serves in its entirety as so much saleable matter. Spread on a canvas, with other paints around it, it represents, on the contrary, a feature in a picture and performs a spiritual function. Just so, I maintain, does a given undivided portion of experience, taken in one context of associates, play the part of a knower, of a state of mind, of "consciousness"; while in a different context the same undivided bit of experience plays the part of a thing known, of an objective "content." In a word, in one group it figures as a thought, in another group as a thing. And, since it can figure in both groups simultaneously we have every right to speak of it as subjective and objective both at once.[26]

The "pure experience" view needs a fuller statement before we can properly examine it. This statement we can postpone. For the present it need only be pointed out that this view does indeed solve James's epistemological problems. It gets rid of the difficulty of how an idea—a mental thing—can know an object—a physical thing—by reducing each of them to a single substance—pure experience. This eliminates the difference in kind between mind and matter and gives us an epistemological monism as well as a metaphysical monism. By making mind a function of a stream of experiences—that is, mind is simply the experiences taken in one way—and matter a function of another sequence of experiences—the experiences taken in another way—we eliminate mind and matter as self-subsistent entities. Thus at one bold stroke we undercut the mind-body problem as well as eliminating mind and matter as unknown somewhats—unexperienced substrata of the physical and mental world.

A further epistemological advantage—and one which James probably valued more than all the rest—was that by having a world made up solely of experiences, a knower could move around freely and smoothly in any direction without the saltatory leap which a dichotomy in the nature of mind and body required. By thus making ambulation as a knowledge process fully possible, James provided an underpinning which supported and strengthened his whole epistemology. His view of the knowledge process required that each succeeding idea of the object should bring us closer and closer to it. A world of pure experience made such ambulation possible. As an ideal limit, complete knowledge was to be attained when the series of steps terminated in an experience which was identical with—merged with—the known object. If the object was itself an experience—as the pure-experience view made it—then this final merging was possible and the ideal limit was a real possibility even though we might never know when we had reached it.

Another interesting problem that was handled well by this view was that of a theory of error. A theory of error is the other side of the coin from a theory of truth. A theory of truth must show how truth can be obtained; a theory of error must explain how error can occur. The history of epistemology is littered with the wrecks of theories of knowledge that foundered on one or the other of these. Theories which account for truth cannot explain error and those which explain error cannot account for truth. In brief, a theory of truth that says we have direct knowledge of an object makes it possible to have true knowledge of it. But if our knowledge is direct and immediate, how is it possible for us to err and be mistaken? To allow for error we then introduce between the knowing mind and the object known a mediating element—the sense experience—which represents the object to the mind. We then explain error by saying that when error occurs it is because the sense image misrepresented the object. But if all our knowledge of the object is mediated by sense experiences, then all we ever know is the sense experiences and the object remains forever beyond our epistemological grasp. Thus the direct-experience type of theory allows us to explain truth but makes it impossible to account for error; the indirect experience theory—the object known by means of a representation—explains error but eliminates the possibility of truth. James's theory of pure experience obviates this difficulty by allowing for error in the ambulatory steps which take us to the object, and makes truth possible by holding that the final term in the series of experiences is the object which when that final term is reached is known directly and immediately with a completeness that makes absolute truth possible.

A final problem that James's epistemology had to deal with was the question of whether there was such a thing as real relations which joined things together. His ambulatory process required conjunctions if the knower was to move about the world smoothly and easily. Ever since David Hume's famous dictum in the eighteenth century that all sense experiences were "loose and separate," there had been an increasing tendency on the part of empiricists in epistemology to atomize the universe of knowledge. After thus breaking it into parts, the problem was how to put it back together again. If all sense experiences were "loose and separate," how could one sense experience "know" another, for instance? How could it remember and connect itself with other experiences? The whole tissue of knowledge was shredded by the belief that the only "real" relations were disjunctive relations. Conjunctive relations—connections between things—were products of the knowing mind, not of the real relation of things to one another. Hume's separation of causes from effects made this way of thinking seem plausible. The associationist psychologies of the nineteenth century with their assertion that associations were made by the mind supported this view.

All of this made knowledge impossible. In the sense that knowledge is a prediction, it must establish a connection between a present cause and a future effect. It must know connections between past and present in order to provide guides for the future. If there are no connections at all, if the world is simple chaos, then knowledge is indeed impossible since of a chaos nothing can be known except that it is indeed a chaos.

James grasped this thorn firmly. He held that conjunctive relations existed and were as real as disjunctive relations. This was why he chose as a name for his epistemology the term "radical" empiricism. Other empiricists did not go far enough to suit him. They were not thoroughgoing; they did not see that experience showed conjunctions as well as disjunctions.

Both James's pragmatism and his theory of truth required him to assert that connections were real. In the pragmatic view an idea is a prediction that if we act in a certain manner we will have certain experiences. There is asserted here a connection between our idea and its practical consequences as well as a connection within the practical consequence between the action and the percept. If these connections are illusions, then our ideas are fictions and we know nothing about the world. Further, in James's view, truth is that property of an idea which asserts that there is a relation of satisfactory-working between the idea of the object and the object. If this conjunctive relation is not real, then truth is an illusion.

James thought that experience actually showed connections. When I hear a bell stroke and then a second bell stroke, I really hear it as a second bell stroke. It is not isolated from the first one. The experience is really of it as a second stroke—as being related conjunctively to a previous experience. When I see things in space I see them as related to one another in space. One of them is to the left of the other one. They are really related in this way. They are connected by the relation and I experience the real relation. "Radical empiricism takes conjunctive relations at their face value, holding them to be as real as the terms united by them. The world it represents as a collection, some parts of which are conjunctively and other parts disjunctively related."[27]

In the preface to his *The Meaning of Truth,* James summarized his radical empiricism in a way that should now be clear to the reader:

Radical empiricism consists first of a postulate, next of a statement of fact, and finally of a generalized conclusion.

The postulate is that the only things that shall be debatable among philosophers shall be things definable in terms drawn from experience. (Things of an unexperienceable nature may exist ad libitum, but they form no part of the material for philosophic debate.)

The statement of fact is that the relations between things, conjunctive as well as disjunctive, are just as much matters of direct particular experience, neither more so nor less so, than the things themselves.

The generalized conclusion is that therefore the parts of experience hold together from next to next by relations that are themselves parts of experience. The directly apprehended universe needs, in short, no extraneous trans-empirical connective support, but possesses in its own right a concatenated or continuous structure.[28]

While James's radical empiricism required that he believe in connections or conjunctions as real, the belief in connections could also be carried too far for his purposes. A philosopher might argue that rather than nothing being connected, everything was connected. Under these latter circumstances the world would be all of one piece, everything would be connected to everything else, we would have one big united hunk of stuff, what James called a "block-universe." Opposed to this notion of a block-universe James developed what he called a "pluriverse" rather than a "universe." Rather than a monism, a one, there was a many, a plurality of things. Some of these things were connected; others were not.

The notion of a monism was popular in James's day with some noted philosophers. It had been developed in detail by James's Harvard colleague in philosophy Josiah Royce in his *The World and the Individual,* and by the British philosopher F. H. Bradley in his book *Appearance and Reality.* The doctrine had a number of forms. First, it had a theological form. God, being omniscient, knew everything, therefore everything was "one," was related at a minimum, by being known by one knower, God. God not only knew everything present, but he knew the past and the future as well. He had created everything, therefore it was one in having been created by him. He had created it for a purpose of his, and it was therefore one through a unity of purpose. The entire scheme of things was connected through God, the ultimate principle and ground of all things.

This theological version was rewritten by Royce and Bradley so as to remove the anthropomorphic features. It became a purely metaphysical principle, a consciousness in which everything existed. In this guise it became "the Absolute."

The Absolute obviously encouraged a metaphysical idealism. If everything was part of the Absolute, then it had as its essential nature a spiritual and conscious force which did not set well with the notion of a universe made up of matter. Matter was too gross and clumsy as the base for such a universe. An objective idealism, on the other hand, made a universe of mind, or idea, which was easily infused with the kind of spiritual quality connoted by the notion of an Absolute.

This idealism easily became a "transcendental idealism"—one which held that knowledge was not to be found in the world of sense experience but only by "transcending" the world of the senses to a more ultimate reality. The world of the senses was vague and contradictory and, particularly, it was irrational. It could not be "understood," it just was. There was a "brute" element in the world of experience which eluded the efforts of the intellect to grasp it—and of what use to a philosopher was a world that could not be "understood." James quotes Bradley as saying of the facts of experience: "I find that my intellect rejects [them] because they contradict themselves. They offer a complex of diversities conjoined in a way which it feels is not its way and which it cannot repeat as its own. . . . For to be satisfied, my intellect must understand, and it can not understand by taking a congeries in the lump."[29]

Since, for the transcendental idealist, the world "must" be rational, such that we can "understand" it, sense experience cannot be the ultimate ground of things. There must be something beyond sense experience in which the contradictions of sense experience are resolved and its irrationality disappears. To really "know" the world, then, the philosopher must "transcend" the senses—go beyond them to an ultimate reality that is rational and that can be known only to the reason. The world of the senses is a world of appearance; the ultimate reality transcends this appearance.

For this transcendent reality to be known it must be "knowable." We have referred above to the difficulty in the mind-body problem revolving around the question of how a mind could fully "know" something (matter) that was nonmental in nature. The accepted verdict was that mind could not know matter. Therefore, if the transcendent reality was knowable, it would have itself to be of the nature of mind or idea. This led again to a metaphysics of idealism which, since it was transcendent, provided a world that could not be known by sense experience but which, since it was an idealism, could be known by reason. It therefore satisfied the requirement of being understandable, at least in theory if not in fact.

This transcendental reality was still not necessarily a unity, however. An argument was necessary to show that the multiplicity of things was only an appearance, that reality was one, a unity. The argument here was carried on at the level of logic. Since we had by now reached the point that sense experience could not reveal reality, there was obviously no point in referring to it for adjudication of the issue. If reality was rational it was logical, and logic should then be the method to be resorted to in metaphysics.

The logical question at issue was expressed as the doctrine of internal relations versus the doctrine of external relations. The doctrine of internal relations held that everything and anything in the universe was ultimately and intimately "related to everything else." Things were related internally if a change in the relation made a simultaneous change in the things related.[30]

For example, in an intricate device like a watch or an electric motor, an alteration in the spatial relations (the position) of the parts would affect the behavior of the watch or motor and of the parts. The parts are, then, internally related. Thus in an automobile engine, the spatial relation of the spark plugs to the cylinders is, logically, an internal one. If we remove the spark plugs from their sockets they no longer function as spark plugs, the cylinders do not function as cylinders, and the engine does not function as an engine. The relation of these various components, then, is an internal one, logically, since a change in the relation changes the objects involved. The spark plugs cease being spark plugs and become simply oddly shaped pieces of metal.

But are all relations internal? If I have the spark plugs sitting on top of the left fender while I work on the motor, and I move them from there to the right fender to get them out of the way, does this change, from left-fenderness to right-fenderness, affect the spark plugs? Does it alter their nature? In short, is it an internal relation or an external relation? Common sense would say that it is an external relation. But not so says transcendental idealism. All things are internally related. Any change in the relation of anything makes a change in the nature of everything—including that thing. If changes in spatial relations do not appear to make a change in things, then so much the worse for spatial relations: they must be an illusion, a property of the world of senses, an "appearance." Similarly with time relations. Since many changes in time do not appear to affect the things which stand in that relation—the spark plugs do not appear to be different from one second to the next—then time also must be an appearance. Transcendent reality is outside of time and space. It does not change, since change involves an alteration in time or space. It is one, absolute, complete, and unalterable.

That there are no external relations, that any change in the relations must make a change in what is related and thus be internal, is argued by Bradley, who admits that:

> . . . such external relations seem possible and even existing. . . . That you do not alter what you compare or rearrange in space seems to common sense quite obvious, and that on the other side there are obvious difficulties does not occur to common sense at all. And I will begin by pointing out these difficulties. . . . There is a relation in the result, and this relation, we hear, is to make no difference in its terms. But, if so, to what does it make a difference and what is the meaning and sense of qualifying the term by it? If, in short, it is external to the terms, how can it possibly be true of them? . . . If the terms from their inner natures do not enter into the relations, then, so far as they are concerned, they seem related for no reason at all. . . . Things are spatially related, first in one way, and then become related in another way, and yet in no way themselves are altered; for the relations, it is said, are but external. But I reply that, if so, I can not *understand* the leaving by the terms of one set of relations

and their adoption of another fresh set. The process and its result to the terms, if they contribute nothing to it, seem irrational throughout. But, if they contribute anything, they must surely be affected internally. . . . That for working purposes we treat, and do well to treat, some relations as external merely I do not deny, and that of course is not the question at issue here. That question is . . . whether in the end and in principle a mere external relation is possible. . . .[31]

Of course, if external relations are not possible, then all there are are internal relations. Everything then is intimately related to everything else and the universe is, by the intimacy of these relations, welded firmly into a single whole, a unity, a block-universe.

James found himself, again, in his metaphysics, seeking to mediate between two extremes. There was, on the one side, the view of the traditional empiricist that everything in the universe was "loose and separate," that nothing was connected with anything else. At the other extreme was the view of the rationalist that nothing was loose and separate, that everything was connected with everything else.*

In seeking a middle ground here, in promoting a universe in which some things were intimately connected and others not, James was doing a number of things. He was fully rejecting the absolutes of his Calvinistic upbringing for one thing—as we shall see shortly in his religious metaphysics. He was affirming his faith in the method of science—a method which found some real connections (scientific laws) in the world, and hence was

---

* The former view was embodied in Chauncey Wright's metaphor of the universe as cosmic weather, the latter view in Josiah Royce's absolute idealism.

not a form of Hume's "loose and separate" empiricism —and thereby rejecting "pure reason" as the method of understanding the world. And he was allying himself with a metaphysical view of the universe as an open universe, a view which was shared by the other members of the pragmatist-humanist group: Charles Peirce, John Dewey, and F. C. S. Schiller.

To reach his own metaphysics James combined a number of concepts. Some of these he developed himself, some he borrowed. But on all of them he left his own imprint. These elements include pure experience, a pluralistic universe, novelty, meliorism, evolutionary progress, and a finite god. Some of these elements we have already discussed. It may be well to review them in connection with James's metaphysics.

James comes to the doctrine of pure experience probably for the same reasons other nineteenth-century philosophers came to idealism. That is, there seems no other way to deal with the mind-body problem as an epistemological issue. If mind and body were really different in nature, knowledge of matter by mind seemed forever impossible. The world, then, had to be one or the other. Materialism, the view that only matter exists, would not solve the problem. Aside from the patent fact that we are all conscious—so that consciousness or mind exists in some sense—to show how a lifeless and inert stuff like matter could "know" other bodies seemed even more difficult than it did to show how mind could do it.*

James was not an idealist of the transcendental variety

---

* Thus we find Charles Peirce writing in the 1890's that "the old dualistic notion of mind and matter, so prominent in Cartesianism, as two radically different kinds of substance, will hardly find defenders today. Rejecting this, we are driven to some form of . . . monism. . . . The one intelligible theory of the universe is that of objective idealism. . . ." (*Collected Papers*, 6.24, 25)

—his view was constantly criticized for being too subjective. But it would seem as though he could quite properly have been a subjective idealist of the Berkeleian variety. He believed in real external objects. But so, in his own way, did Berkeley. The differences between James's view and that of Berkeley would be difficult to find so far as external objects are concerned. In one discussion of Berkeley's view, James says:

> Berkeley's criticism of "matter" was consequently absolutely pragmatistic. Matter is known as our sensations of colour, figure, hardness and the like. They are the cash value of the term. The difference matter makes to us by truly being is that we then get such sensations; by not being, is that we lack them. These sensations then are its sole meaning. Berkeley doesn't deny matter, then; he simply tells us what it consists of. It is a true name for just so much in the way of sensations.[32]

For both James and Berkeley, to say that material objects exist is to say that we have certain sense experiences. Matter as an unexperienced *Ding an sich* does not have any part in the philosophy of either of them. The primary difference between their views would seem to lie in Berkeley's ascribing God as the origin of our ideas and James ascribing "pure experience" as the only thing that underlies our ideas. A second significant difference would come from Berkeley following a traditional empiricist view that sensations come as separated sensations. It is in fact the metaphysical reincarnation of the "stream of consciousness" which he pronounced as a psychologist. It operates at the level of what we would call "percepts," but it is continuous and objective, rather than discrete and subjective. He refers to it as "the perceptual flux"[33] and describes it in a classic passage as follows:

"Pure experience" is the name which I gave to the immediate flux of life which furnishes the material to our later reflection with its conceptual categories. Only new-born babes, or men in semi-coma from sleep, drugs, illnesses, or blows, may be assumed to have an experience pure in the literal sense of a *that* which is not yet any definite *what,* tho' ready to be all sorts of whats; full both of oneness and of manyness, but in respects that don't appear; changing throughout, yet so confusedly that its phases interpenetrate and no points, either of distinction or of identity, can be caught. Pure experience in this state is but another name for feeling or sensation. But the flux of it no sooner comes than it tends to fill itself with emphases, and these salient parts become identified and fixed and abstracted; so that experience now flows as if shot through with adjectives and nouns and prepositions and conjunctions. Its purity is only a relative term, meaning the proportional amount of unverbalized sensation which it still embodies.[34]

This pure experience is the basic stuff of which everything is made. It is conscious, although not self-conscious, so we have a form of panpsychism. But it is not God, so we do not have a pantheism. It is the basic continuum, a flux of experience, prior to any distinction of God, self, consciousness, material object, space, time, etc.

We have discussed the sense in which pure experience may become either a mind or a material object. If taken in one sequence it is a material object. If taken in another sequence it is a mind. Some experiences taken from one perspective are part of the history of a material object, a table; the same experiences taken from another perspective are part of the history of a mental object, my conscious self.

Two important new points are now to be noted. First of all, the material object and the self do not exist per se. They are simply the pure experience taken in different sequences. They are the sequences, so to speak, not the contents of the sequence. For this reason a second point comes to view: the *same* portion of pure experience can be in one sequence as part of the table and in another sequence as part of a self. The pure experience is not "swallowed up" by one sequence to the exclusion of others. The reader may recall the illustration we used earlier of an event occurring at a street intersection. An event taken in the "Main Street sequence" could *at the same time* be taken in the "Jones Avenue sequence." We may generalize the illustration by saying that a point may be found simultaneously on two lines if the lines intersect. Furthermore, an infinite number of lines may be drawn through any given point, so that the same point may simultaneously be part of an unlimited number of sequences. Thus a number of knowers may in fact know the same thing because they know simultaneously the same piece of pure experience. The same piece may in fact be simultaneously a part of the sequence that makes up a physical object and a number of minds.

Finally, one of these knowers may be a sequence which is more all-inclusive than the rest, more percipient or more perfect. This sequence may be what we mean by God. Thus the same bit of pure experience may simultaneously be part of a physical object, several human minds, and God's mind. But the physical object, the human knowers, and God are not entities in themselves, but only certain sequences cut out of the flux. They are different statues seen in the same piece of marble.

From this same flux with its sequences we get a pluralistic universe. Not all the sequences will have points in common. Some will be completely separated from others so that no intersection of any kind occurs. They will have no possibility of internal relations. They will continue a many, a plurality of things not yet united in any way. Perhaps they may become united. But as we now know them they do not present themselves as united even in God's experience.

In such a flux where new sequences occur and new conjunctions of old sequences are made, new and previously unseen things occur. We have a chance for novelty in the pluriverse.

The novelty which James sought for his universe was found by him in perceptual experience. No portion of the flux was ever exactly identical with another portion. There was always something different and new in each experience. "Time keeps budding into new moments, every one of which presents a content which in its individuality never was before and will never be again. Of no concrete bit of experience was any exact duplicate ever framed."[35]

This newness in experience provided a continual opportunity to rebuild the universe. Like biological mutations, the cosmological mutations could be accumulated and built out in definite directions. If one selected the right directions he could make a better world for himself and his fellows. If he picked the wrong direction the result would be a worse world. But the choice as to the direction things would go was not predetermined from all eternity. The end was open, it was undetermined. We had then an "open universe," wending whither we know not, except that we discern that creative selection by conscious choices helps decide on ends: "If we look at the general mass of things in the midst of which the life of men is passed, and ask 'How came they here?' the only broad answer is that man's desires preceded and produced them. . . . Human causal activity is the only known unconditional antecedent of the works of civilization . . ."[36]

If the universe is open, if what it is to become is not determined, then we have the possibility of helping to decide its conclusion. Such a doctrine would be different from the traditional views of pessimism or optimism.

Pessimism says that the world is so structured that it must necessarily end in nothing. The fate of man and the universe is determined, for example, by the second law of thermodynamics, which says clearly that all usable forms of energy must someday be used up and that man with his higher hopes and aspirations must return to the abyss from which he came. This is the thoroughgoing scientific view which James labeled as tough-minded.

Optimism says that the world is so structured that it must necessarily end in the triumph of spiritual over merely material forces. In its religious form, for example, optimism says that the world's salvation is inevitable. Although in the physical world pain and death and destruction do occur, physical life is followed by a spiritual life in which these things are surmounted and we live in a state of permanent bliss.

James could not rest easy in either of these alternatives. Pessimism did not offer enough and optimism offered too much. He wanted a world in which nothing was guaranteed—the world was not necessarily going to end in destruction or bliss—and he wanted a world in which the outcome was decided, at least in part, by human efforts. To this general attitude he gave the name of meliorism.[37] This was to be the view that salvation was neither necessary nor impossible. It is possible to make a world in which man is saved and the finer values are preserved, but it is not guaranteed and it is only even possible if we all work together.

Suppose the world's author put the case to you before creation, saying: "I am going to make a world not certain to be saved, a world the perfection of which shall be conditional merely, the condition being that each several agent does its own 'level best.' I offer you the chance of taking part in such a world. Its safety, you see, is unwarranted. It is a real adventure, with real danger, yet it may win through. It is a social scheme of co-operative work genuinely to be done. Will you join the procession? Will you trust yourself and trust the other agents enough to face the risk?"[38]

The tender-minded, who feel the need for peace and security, would not accept such a universe. Nor would the tough-minded, who see such a possibility as mere wishful thinking. But for those who want a middle view —as James did—it would provide exactly what was needed. It was the view he began searching for at the start of his intellectual life and it satisfied him at the end.

Such a view eliminated the absolute deity of traditional theism in the same way that James's metaphysics rejected the absolute of transcendental idealism. Since any god that existed must not know the final end of the universe—since it was an open universe—he was not omniscient. Since he must not be able completely to reach a satisfactory goal by himself—otherwise human effort would be redundant and without a significance—he was not omnipotent.

That there was such a limited, or finite, God, James called the religious hypothesis of humanism or pragmatism. He saw the universe as containing the possibility of a higher form of consciousness than ours.

> I believe rather that we stand in much the same relation to the whole of the universe as our canine and feline pets do to the whole of human life. They inhabit our drawing-rooms and libraries. They take part in scenes of whose significance they have no inkling. . . . But, just as many of the dogs' and cats' ideals coincide with our ideals, . . . so we may well believe, on the proofs that religious experience affords, that higher powers exist and are at work to save the world on lines similar to our own.[39]

James felt that as a pragmatist he could not assert that such a religious hypothesis was true—that religious hypothesis would be true which proved to work best in the widest sense and in the long run—but he thought there was some evidence for it in the religious experiences of mystics (collected at length in his *The Varieties of Religious Experience*) and in the various forms of activity reported by spiritualistic mediums.

> . . . the drift of all the evidence we have seems to me to sweep us very strongly towards the belief in some form of superhuman life with which we may, unknown to ourselves, be co-conscious. . . .
> . . . the only way to escape from the paradoxes and perplexities that a consistently thought-out monistic universe suffers from as from a species of auto-intoxication—the mystery of the "fall" namely, of reality lapsing into appearance, truth into error, perfection into imperfection; of evil, in short; the mystery of universal determinism, of the block-universe eter-

nal and without a history, etc.;—the only way of escape, I say, from all this is to be frankly pluralistic and assume that the superhuman consciousness, however vast it may be, has itself an external environment, and consequently is finite . . . that there is a God, but that he is finite, either in power or in knowledge, or in both at once.[40]

There is no doubt that James was swept to this finite God by the struggles he encountered in his youth with the problems of evil and free will, and in maturity with transcendental idealism. He says of the finite religious perspective: "My primary reason for advocating it is its matchless intellectual economy. It gets rid, not only of the standing 'problems' that monism engenders ('problem of evil,' 'problem of freedom,' and the like), but of other metaphysical mysteries and paradoxes as well."[41]

With an omniscient, omnipotent God, evil could not really exist. Such a God would know how to get rid of it and would be able to. Being benevolent, he would do so. The only possible conclusion from this perspective is that (non-man-caused) evil does not exist. What seems to us to be evil is not. When seen in the whole scheme of things the evil will become an appearance and the event will turn out to be really good. The evil is swallowed up, then, when seen from the eternal perspective of an absolute deity.

James was not willing to see evil this way. There seemed to him no way to explain much of the pain and suffering in the world except as genuinely evil, and as evil from any perspective. Such evil, then, was not to be accounted as good, but was to be seen for what it was as an evil, and was to be overcome. So that in overcoming evil we were not simply transforming one good (that "appeared" evil) into another good, but rather were overcoming a real evil and making of it a good. This meant that our efforts did count for something in the struggle. All was not pre-determined from all eternity and pre-known by an all-knower. Our struggle to overcome evil and ignorance represents a genuine struggle, not a mock warfare. Where we succeed, something of significance has been accomplished.

If God is not omnipotent, then, he may be able to understand the evil but unable to conquer it. In such a case our help might be useful. Or, if he is not omniscient, he may be able to overcome the evil but not know how to do so. Again assistance may be helpful. In either case evil is not an illusion, God is not responsible for it, genuine victory of good is possible, and human efforts are significant in attaining the victory.

Such a deity is not only helped by us but also helps us. "The believer finds that the tenderer parts of his personal life are continuous with a *more* of the same quality which is operative in the universe outside of him and which he can keep in working touch with, and in a fashion get on board of and save himself, when all his lower being has gone to pieces in the wreck. In a word, the believer is continuous, to his own consciousness, at any rate, with a wider self from which saving experiences flow in."[42]

All of James's religious metaphysics was epitomized in his statement about his finite God that "He helps us and we can help him."[43]

We may summarize James's metaphysics in its largest sweep. It begins with a world of "pure experience." Where does the pure experience come from? For James this is like asking: "Where does everything come from?" If "everything" includes everything, then there is nothing outside of it to be its cause. He tells us:

The essential service of humanism, as I conceive the situation, is to have seen that *though one part of our experience may lean upon another part to make it what it is in any one of several aspects in which it may be considered, experience as a whole is self-containing and leans on nothing.*[44]

And so we have as a beginning of the whole scheme of things a flux of pure experience. The flux is not pantheistic in a number of ways, but most significantly in that the total flux is not enveloped in any single consciousness. "Since the acquisition of conscious quality on the part of an experience depends upon a context coming to it, it follows that the sum total of all experiences, having no context, can not strictly be called conscious at all."[45]

Whether James's views should be referred to as panpsychic or not would hinge largely on how much "life" a bit of pure experience would need to have to be alive or "psychic." Essentially what James seems to want to say is that these bits all possess the possibility of life, but they do not realize this possibility except in the context of a series constituting a conscious being. "On the principles which I am defending, a 'mind' or 'personal consciousness' is the name for a series of experiences run together by certain definite transitions. . . ."[46] "To be 'conscious' means not simply to be, but to be reported, known, to have awareness of one's being added to that being . . ."[47]

How or why these contexts, these relations between experiences, occur, we do not know. "How or why the experiences ever *get themselves made,* or *why* their characters and relations are just such as appear, we can not begin to understand."[48]

However, if what we mean by consciousness is a certain

kind of sequence of experiences, then the possibility of such a sequence existing must have been present from the beginning. "If evolution is to work smoothly, consciousness in some shape must have been present at the very origin of things."[49]

In a universe where such sequences are possible, they need not occur by any fiat or by any logical necessity. But they may occur by chance: "Series of independent origin and purpose may inosculate by 'chance-encounter,' and thereafter mingle their causalities and combine their effects."[50]

In such a universe among the series which occur may be some of larger scale and sweep than others. They may include more and take as parts lesser series which they include within themselves. Such a more inclusive series may be what we mean by God. "If evolution, Gods may be one of the results."[51]

The totality of sequences may be increasing their unity by showing a tendency to combine, so that as an ultimate result we may see everything as moving toward or into a single unity. "The world is in so far forth a pluralism of which the unity is not fully experienced as yet . . . the unity of the world is on the whole undergoing increase . . . these very new experiences often help the mass to a more consolidated form."[52]

Thus the universe moves, by an evolutionary process, out of a many into a unity. In this process the most significant unities occur in the vicinity of conscious minds, which demonstrate a creative function by unifying and organizing. Unifications occur mechanically in physical sequences, but creatively and "organically" in the purposive organization of experiences by conscious minds. So that the melioristic universe is a picture of unrelated bits of pure experience being organized into increasingly more all-encompassing sequences by the creative activity of conscious minds—both large and small (i.e., both divine and human)—moving by their joint efforts toward a unity in which all may be included.

First there is solar, and then there is geological evolution, processes accurately describable as integrations in the mechanical sense, namely, as decrease in bulk, or growth in hardness. Then life appears; and after that neither integration of matter nor dissipation of motion plays any part whatever. The result of life, however, is to fill the world more and more and more with things displaying *organic unity*. By this is meant any arrangement of which one part helps to keep the other parts in existence. Some organic unities are material—a sea urchin, for example, a department store, a civil service, or an ecclesiastical organization. Some are mental, as a "science," a code of laws, or an educational programme. But whether they be material or mental products, organic unities must accumulate; for every old one tends to conserve itself and if successful new ones arise they also "come to stay."[53]

With this description of James's metaphysics in mind it is possible to throw some helpful light on a number of points in his philosophy that have been bothersome to his critics. The key to understanding much that is strange in James is this metaphysics of a universe "in the making." Most of Western philosophy comes in just the opposite metaphysics. Philosophers trained in that latter tradition continue to find James's position a difficult one. Most of us are what James called by various names but commonly referred to as intellectualists. He tells us that " 'Intellectualism' is the belief that our mind comes upon a world complete in itself, and has the duty of ascertaining its contents; but has no power of re-determining its character, for that is already given."[54]

Even though Western philosophy has recognized an element of change in the physical world, this change has been swallowed up, so to speak, by an omniscient deity. The world may appear to you and me to change, but God, who sees it at every instant from all eternity to all eternity, has, and has always had, complete foreknowledge of things from the beginning to the end. In his mind, then, all lies known and previsioned. The changing stages which the physical world appears to go through are simply successive moments in an already completely laid out plan. Since this plan was completely laid out at the beginning of things, it follows that from the perspective of God the scheme of the universe was finished before it began. In such a universe no real change would be possible. Nothing new could come into existence because everything was already anticipated. All that could happen would be the unfolding of a previously conceived plan. From this perspective all the problems that were bothersome to James—the problem of evil, the problem of free will—sweep back upon us.

Similarly, in such a view, man's efforts contribute nothing. The struggle to make a better world is a farce. What is going to happen is already foreknown by God and nothing else can happen. Man thinks that by his efforts he helps determine the outcome, but the outcome was already settled before he appeared on the scene.

In such a world there is nothing for a philosopher to do but to seek to "know" the universe, to seek to comprehend or grasp an already completed scheme of things. If he attains such knowledge he then fulfills his philosophical duty. In this situation the world is given, it is presented to him finished and completed. He does not act upon it but only seeks to understand it. We have what

John Dewey came to call a "spectator theory of knowledge." The human knower is a passive spectator watching the unfolding of a drama in which he has no part.

Contrast this with James's view in which the human being is not a spectator to the drama but an actor—or more literally even, one of the authors. The contrast between the two views is quite as sharp a difference as that between being a member of the audience and being an actor-author. As a member of the audience, the philosopher's only job would be to "understand" the drama. As an actor-author his job is to help create the drama. He contributes to determining its final outcome. His efforts are significant and valuable.

The first and sharpest difference between the philosopher in these two roles is that in the former he is passive and in the latter he is active. This activist element in James's thought is reflected in his pragmatism. The philosopher is not "man thinking" but "man acting." He must abandon his ivory-tower role and move down into the market place of practical affairs. This change in roles was more of a traumatic experience than many of James's philosophic contemporaries could subscribe to.

When the philosopher in his new role functions as a student of ethics, he does so no longer simply as someone seeking to understand an already completed notion of good and duty. He searches instead among the practical day-to-day lives of men to cull out nuggets of what seem to be good things. He seeks to weave about them a web of theory prescribing modes of behavior which when acted upon will make these goods secure for all men. He projects this theory as a hypothesis for testing in the world of affairs. So far as it proves useful, men adopt it; so far as it does not, it is rejected and revised. In a universe in the making, goods are one of the things that get made.

The philosopher in this new role has a similar relation

to knowledge. The world does not consist of already completed objects which he seeks to know as they write their sensory messages on his passive *tabula rasa*. The philosopher acts on the world. His actions have effect. They change the world. They make things, new things previously unheard of. From atom bombs to earth satellites, men literally construct a world. The world is made by our efforts. Its future is a function of the choices we make and the things we do.

Finally, man in this new perspective takes on a new dignity. Rather than being a participant in a drama he never made, he becomes one of the creators of things. His efforts count, his victories are valuable, his errors tragic. By attaining effectiveness he attains responsibility. If things fail, he must bear at least part of the blame; if they succeed, he merits at least part of the credit.

It is now possible to see some of what James means when he calls his view a religious hypothesis. It is one of several such views about the nature of man, God, and the universe. In common with the other alternative hypotheses, it must be tested. To be tested it must be tried, it must be believed and lived. Those to whom it appeals emotionally have a right to believe it and live it. By so doing they are putting it to a test. If it succeeds, if it proves a useful way of living, it will be adopted by others. If it proves fruitless, it will be discarded. "If theological ideas prove to have a value for concrete life, they will be true. . . ."[55]

Thus James gets to the paradox of his "faith-ladder," which allows him to say of a view which is not logically impossible but is emotionally appealing that "it *might* have been true, it *may* be true, it is *fit* to be true, it *ought* to be true, it *must* be true, it *shall* be true for *me*."[56] Such a believer is putting his faith to the test. He is staking his all on it. He ought to be admired rather than con- demned.

If James is right, if this is a world that is in the mak- ing, then his other views follow. Faith must run before the fact, because our beliefs help decide what the facts are going to be. Whether we believe in a God or not may be a more important matter than the agnostic recognizes, because what God becomes—or whether gods come at all —may depend upon what we believe now. In such a world truth will grow and change. Reality will be affected by what man and God do to the flux of things. And man and God will in turn be affected by what they do to things.

Such a view of the universe may not be appealing to many. And to many of James's critics it remained unap- pealing. But it is not logically inconsistent or epistemo- logically impossible. It is a new and forthright statement of one of the alternatives among religious metaphysics. It deserves a better hearing among philosophers than it has yet received.

In his later years James saw that his was the generation of Western man for whom a great change in religious out- look had taken place. In 1909, in the opening pages of *A Pluralistic Universe,* he described the intellectual change of life that he had lived through. In it he described the transition from Calvinism to Darwinism which the thinkers of his time had had to make. In summarizing this change he recapitulated his own life's thought and experience in religion:

Those of us who are sexagenarians have witnessed in our own persons one of the gradual mutations of intellectual climate, due to innumerable influences, that make the thought of a past generation seem as foreign to its successor as if it were the expression of a different race of men. The theological machinery that spoke so livingly to our ancestors, with its finite age of the world, its creation out of nothing, its juridicial morality and eschatology, its relish for rewards and punishments, its treatment of God as an external contriver, an "intelligent and moral governor," sounds as odd to most of us as if it were some outlandish savage religion. The vaster vistas which scientific evolutionism has opened, and the rising tide of social democratic ideals have changed the type of our imagination, and the older monarchical theism is obsolete or obsolescent. The place of the divine in the world must be more organic and intimate. An external creator and his institutions may still be verbally confessed at church in formulas that linger by their mere inertia, but the life is out of them, we avoid dwelling on them, the sincere heart of us is elsewhere.[57]

Chapter 5

EPISTEMOLOGY:
PURE EXPERIENCE IN AN OPEN UNIVERSE

Interesting though James's metaphysics was, it did not win many adherents except in the general way of contributing to the increasing secularization of American philosophy. The wave of the future was to be in epistemology. Here James exerted a powerful influence. An interest in epistemology was initiated by him among American philosophers that was to permeate the New Realist–Critical Realist Movement of the 1920's and was to join forces with the new positivism that came to this country from Europe in the 1930's. Together pragmatism and positivism were to determine the course of American philosophy up to the present.

The pragmatic-positivistic emphasis in American philosophy since James may be thought of as a philosophical form of anti-intellectualism, if by intellectualism we mean armchair speculative philosophy of the sort for which philosophers both in this country and abroad were so notorious in the nineteenth century. Thick volumes of speculative metaphysics have been replaced in the twentieth century by thin volumes of symbolic logic and linguistic analysis. Philosophers are, however, beginning to feel that while logic and linguistics are important, there may be a middle ground between metaphysics and logical analysis. This present-day battlefield is epistemology. In philosophy, in science, and in social science it has become increasingly evident that a deep insight into the basic epistemological issues is essential to any further progress in these areas.

The turn of the wheel is almost complete, so that the student of William James seems to feel that in reading many contemporary philosophers he is re-reading William James. While there is not necessarily any historical connection between James's views and those of contemporary philosophers, there is, nevertheless, a real identity of point of view. For this reason a close look at James's epistemology is a profitable way to get an introduction to contemporary philosophy.

James's metaphysics might almost be described as an antimetaphysics. He was opposed to so much of the speculative philosophy of his time that his "metaphysics" turns out to be a phenomenalist position. It may be seriously debated as to whether phenomenalism is a metaphysics at all. It may be only an epistemology.

Phenomenalism is primarily the view that all we can know anything about is what an older metaphysics would call the appearances of things. Their sensory effects, so to speak. Thus nothing can be known, and hence nothing can be said, about the existence or nonexistence of any reality which causes them. The similarity of this view to James's "pure experience" is evident. The present chapter will undertake to set forth James's epistemology in somewhat greater detail than was possible before we examined his metaphysics, and then to trace his views into the contemporary context.

The great error in philosophy, as James saw it, was what he called variously rationalism or intellectualism. One of his last definitions of this view said that: " 'Intellectualism' is the belief that our mind comes upon a world complete in itself, and has the duty of ascertaining its contents; but has no power of re-determining its character, for that is already given."[1]

The point about intellectualism, or rationalism, is that it sees the world as complete. The mind does not contribute anything to the world; the mind is only passive. It only comes to "know" a world already given. It is this passive role of the intellect that James objects to. In some quarters—particularly among foreign philosophers—pragmatism is a kind of symbol of American thought. It is usually taken as representative of the American interest in the practical. It is more properly representative of the American interest in the active reorganization and reconstruction of the world. John Dewey's disparagement of the "spectator" view of knowledge and his notion of philosophy as the "reconstruction" of the world show his interest in this theme, which he shared with James— and which both of them considered of far greater significance than any theory of pragmatism. Dewey finally came to refer to his position as "instrumentalism" to emphasize the role of knowledge as an instrument for effectively altering the world.

In this activist sense James and Dewey are, indeed, representatives of American culture. If there is one significant contribution to Western civilization that may be appropriately attributed to Americans of all sorts, it would be that since the first colonists began to cut clearings in the New England wilderness we have looked upon the world as something to be rebuilt nearer to our hearts' desire.

There is a passivity about the world of Plato and Aristotle—the world was there to be understood and comprehended, but when that had been done, man had completed his philosophical destiny. If there was a reconstruction to be done it was, as in Plato's utopia, not a reconstruction of reality—which was changeless and unchangeable—but a reconstruction of man to bring him into harmony with a completed and perfect realm of ideas. From the death of Aristotle until at least the Renaissance, the great tradition of Western thought was that where man and the world were out of joint, the fault was man's and was to be corrected by altering his nature so as to bring him into harmony with the given reality of things.

The contrary notion—that the world is our oyster and that when we are having trouble we operate on the world so as to bring *it* into harmony with *us* and our needs—is a fairly recent one in human history. It begins, perhaps, with Francis Bacon. It does not end with American pragmatism, although it gets a full philosophical treatment there. The notion that man makes his own destiny, that his is not made by it, that he can by knowledge make and remake until the world bears no noticeable resemblance to what was initially given—this notion has grown slowly and steadily in American life. In some other countries of the world it has dropped with explosive force, setting up tensions between the past and the present that have produced revolutions, dictatorships, and terror. New worlds do not come to birth easily. It is not likely that the labor pangs are done yet. But the vision of a world that can be remade by human effort, a world for whose future man is responsible, is surely one of the finest visions of philosophy. This philosophy came from many persons in many places. One of them was William James.

For James the world consists of a flux of pure experience out of which man—by observation and inspiration—carves isolable chunks to which he gives names. These chunks have no identity in reality as chunks. They are simply artificial cuts out of what is in reality a continuum.

Man cuts them out for purposes of thought and purposes of behavior. But the cuts are *his* cuts, not nature's. If a cut seems unsuitable he returns it to the flux from which it came and makes a new cut. But all the time the cuts are his. If he becomes enamored of a cut and forgets that it is his, he may project it onto reality and consider as an attribute of reality what is only an attribute of man.

If he does this the cuts are then reified. They are called ideas or essences. They are made permanent and unchanging. In the flux of sense chaos they are something stable and permanent, something to tie to. Thus the world of concepts, or ideas, gets set off as different from and superior to the world of percepts, or sense experiences. Essentially the transition is completed by treating the concept as embodying the essence, the reality of things, to which the percepts must conform. Thus the concept which began as the servant of the percept ends up as its master. This is what James means by rationalism.

To this rationalist notion of an ideal order of concepts which are immutable and nobler than sense experience, James opposes an empiricist scheme of a world which begins in a welter of sensation out of which artificial— and all too human—concepts are cut.

The cuts we make are purely ideal. If my reader can succeed in abstracting from all conceptual interpretation and lapse back into his immediate sensible life at this very moment, he will find it to be what someone has called a big blooming buzzing confusion. . . .

Out of this aboriginal sensible muchness attention carves out objects, which conception then names and identifies forever—in the sky "constellations," on the earth "beach," "sea," "cliff," "bushes," "grass." Out of time we cut "days" and "nights," "summers" and "winters." We say *what* each part of the sensible continuum is, and all these abstracted *whats* are concepts.[2]

From this analysis of how concepts are formed we are led inevitably to "the empiricist contention that *the significance of concepts consists always in their relation to perceptual particulars. . . .*"[3] "The flux can never be superseded. We must carry it with us to the bitter end of our cognitive business, keeping it in the midst of the translation even when the latter proves illuminating, and falling back on it alone when the translation gives out. 'The insuperability of sensation' would be a short expression of my thesis."[4]

These cuts, or concepts, are class names for a group of percepts. How do we make the cuts that produce the concepts? Are they formed at random or controlled by a purpose? Probably reflecting the Darwinian atmosphere, James sees concepts as being formed under the exigencies of practical needs. "We *harness* perceptual reality in concepts in order to drive it better to our ends."[5]

But if concepts are primarily the ways in which we order the perceptual flux for practical purposes, then it follows that to ascertain the meaning of a concept we have only to discover what bits of the perceptual flux—what sense experiences—it will lead us into when we act upon it in practice. And this is how James arrives at the pragmatic maxim that the meaning of an idea consists in the sense experiences (the percepts) we would expect if we acted upon it.

We thus get a notion of a perceptual flux out of which concepts are cut as maps or guides and which return us to certain percepts which they predict for the future if we act so as to follow the map.

James found this doctrine early in his career. In his *Principles of Psychology* he wrote:

> Conceptual systems which neither began nor left off in sensations would be like bridges without piers. Systems about fact must plunge themselves into sensation as bridges plunge their piers into the rock. Sensations are the stable rock, the *terminus a quo* and the *terminus ad quem* of thought. To find such termini is our aim with all our theories—to conceive first when and where a certain sensation may be had, and then to have it. Finding it stops discussion. Failure to find it kills the false conceit of knowledge. Only when you deduce a possible sensation for me from your theory, and give it to me when and where your theory requires, do I begin to be sure that your thought has anything to do with truth.[6]

Thus we get a view which does not pretend to transcend experience, as much of nineteenth-century philosophy did, but only seeks to step outside of it to see where it is going, so to speak, before plunging back into the stream of sense experience. This insistence upon ideas as guides to future experience is what we have referred to above as "normative" empiricism as distinguished from the "genetic" empiricisms of earlier philosophy. It is this predictive emphasis in James's views which brings him into line with those positions in contemporary philosophy known as positivism and operationalism. While neither positivism nor operationalism is indebted to James, the similarities of the three positions are greater than is ordinarily thought. Thus the British philosopher A. J. Ayer in his book *Language, Truth and Logic,* which is one of the classic formulations of contemporary positivism, tells us that: "Every synthetic [factual] proposition is a rule for the anticipation of future experience, and is distinguished in content from other synthetic propositions by the fact that it is relevant to different siutations."[7] This may be compared with James's statement about the meaning of a concept that ". . . the more important part of its significance may naturally be held to be the consequences to which it leads. . . . If two concepts lead you to infer the same particular consequence, then you may assume that they embody the same meaning under different names."[8]

All of the more recent forms of empiricism—pragmatism, positivism, and operationalism—take this prospective view of knowledge. Traditionally empiricism exhibited a primary concern for the origin of ideas. The genesis of the idea in sense experience, the particular sense impressions from which it came, constituted the content of the idea. For the more recent empiricisms the question has not been where in experience our ideas come from but rather where in experience they go to. Where will they take us? What will they do? They are concerned with the significance of ideas in the literal sense. What does the idea signify? What is it a sign of? What does it stand for or represent in the way of experience?

The traditional view we have labeled above—following Ralph Barton Perry—as genetic empiricism, the latter as normative empiricism. The difference is not merely hortatory. For the genetic empiricist the meaning of an idea, lying as it does in past experience, is something complete and given. The experience has been had, the meaning need only be reached by careful and meticulous analysis of past sense impressions. When patient dissection has laid bare the skeleton of meaning, it can properly be filed away in the appropriate pigeonhole. It is finished. Nothing remains to be done. The Aristotelian essence or the Humean first impression of sense has been reached. On this chapter in the search for meaning the book may be closed.

For the normative empiricist, on the other hand, the meaning of an idea is never "had," it is never complete, it is never finished. The meaning of an idea is a reference to future experiences. These experiences are yet to be known. When they are known they may well be different from what was anticipated, so that the meaning of an idea will change and grow with new experiences. We will never be able to say of an idea that we know all that it means. Absolute knowledge that can be classified and put away as finished can never be attained as long as there remain more human experiences yet to be had.

When normative empiricists undertake to analyze the significance of an idea, they invariably express it in terms of either sense experiences or bodily behaviors or both. Pragmatism, positivism, and operationalism differ primarily as to which of these three alternatives they emphasize. The pragmatist tends to use both perceptions and actions. The positivist relies mainly on perceptions, the operationalist on actions. James tells us that: "To attain perfect clearness in our thought of an object, then, we need only consider . . . what sensations we are to expect from it, and what reactions we must prepare."[9] Hans Reichenbach, speaking from a positivistic position, says that: "A sentence the truth of which cannot be determined from possible observations is meaningless."[10] P. W. Bridgman, the operationalist, says that "the meaning of one's terms are to be found by an analysis of the operations which one performs in applying the term in concrete situations. . . ."[11]

These differences can be easily overstressed, however. As a response to the criticism that operationalism referred meaning solely to physical behaviors, Bridgman asserted that while in his view the content of an idea was a matter of activity on our part, this activity was not all gross physical activity; it could be "either in the perception and recognition by us of sense-impressions, or in the performance by us of deliberate physical manipulation or of deliberate thought."[12]

Related to the normative nature of knowledge in these newer empiricisms is the emphasis on the functional and purposive role of knowledge. Charles Peirce tells us that he chose the name "pragmatism" because of its use by Kant to denote purposive behavior. Peirce says: "Quite the most striking feature of the new theory was its recognition of an inseparable connection between rational cognition and rational purpose; and that consideration it was which determined the preference for the name Pragmatism."[13] Similarly Bridgman proposes classifying operations in terms of their usefulness in attaining our purposes: "Since operations are usually used in a context of purpose of some sort, one may if one likes speak of good or bad operations, but I personally would usually prefer to speak of useful or non-useful operations. It certainly must be recognized that some operations are more useful than others."[14] Reichenbach, in discussing the epistemology of positivism, says: "In contrast to the transcendental conception of knowledge, the philosophy of the new empiricism may be called a *functional conception of knowledge*. In this interpretation, knowledge does not refer to another world, but portrays the things of this world so as to perform a function serving a purpose, the purpose of predicting the future."[15]

The philosophers who have espoused these various forms of normative empiricism have not been unaware of the similarities between their positions. Thus Charles Peirce in 1905 described pragmatism as a form of "prope-positivism," after explaining that by the prefix "prope" he meant "a broad and rather indefinite extension of the meaning of the term."[16]

Dewey recognized a similarity between operationalism and pragmatism so intimate as to lead him to consider them to be identical. In discussing a passage in Eddington's *The Nature of the Physical World,* Dewey wrote:

It is implied in the quotation that concepts are recognized by means of the experimental operations by which they are determined; that is, operations define and test the validity of the meanings by which we state natural happenings. This implication is made explicit a few sentences further along when in speaking of Einstein Mr. Eddington says his theory "insists that each physical quantity should be defined as the result of certain operations of measurement and calculation." The principle is anticipated in Peirce's essay on *How to Make Our Ideas Clear* published as far back as 1881. . . . Peirce states that the sole meaning of the idea of an object consists of the consequences which result when the object is acted upon in a particular way. The principle is one element in the pragmatism of James. The idea is also akin to the "instrumental" theory of conceptions, according to which they are intellectual instruments for directing our activities in relation to existence. . . . On account of ambiguities in the notion of pragmatism —although its *logical* import is identical—I shall follow Bridgman in speaking of "operational thinking."[17]

The similarity between positivism and operationalism has been recognized by Richard Von Mises, who wrote in his book *Positivism:* "P. W. Bridgman, *The Logic of Modern Physics,* 1927, developed, essentially independently of Mach and the Vienna Circle, a consistent, positivistic view of physical concepts and theories. His approach known as operationalism, reduces all acceptable concepts in physics to actions, measurements, operations; it is in close agreement with the point of view represented in this book."[18]

These quotations are indicative of the extent to which these three empirical epistemologies share common approaches. I do not wish to suggest that pragmatism, positivism, and operationalism are identical. But their similarities in epistemology, as distinguished from their differences in ethics and metaphysics, for instance, are sufficiently great that it is certainly not a mistake to identify them as marking a common direction in modern epistemology.

In addition to an orientation toward the future rather than the past as a source of knowledge, another significant difference between normative empiricisms and genetic empiricisms lies in their differing analyses of the problem of the external world. For the genetic empiricist there is a real external world, clearly distinguishable from the world of personal experience. This world is not a world of unknowable Kantian noumena. On the contrary, it reveals itself directly through inspection. Sense experiences are caused by the external reality and are cues, the correct reading of which reveals to the intellect the objective nature of an objective world.

The normative empiricisms, on the other hand, are by no means so straightforward in their assertions about an external reality. For them the problem of an external world becomes a problem in the analysis of language. Where the earlier empiricists posed the straightforward question: "What is the nature of reality?" their later brethren are prone to ask the more sophisticated question: "What do we mean by the *word* 'reality'?" The answer to the latter question turns into an analysis not of the external world but rather of us: "What do *we* mean by our use of our word 'reality'?" The replies to this question vary. The normative empiricist may say that the term "external reality" is empty of meaning. In this case he will assert that metaphysics is cognitively meaningless and may hold with Wittgenstein that "That whereof one cannot speak, of that he must remain silent." Or he may do as Carnap did and treat this as a problem about the logical syntax of language:

It is a pseudo-thesis of idealism and older positivism, that a physical object (*e.g.,* the moon) is a construction out of sense-data. Realism, on the other hand, asserts that a physical object is not constructed but only cognized by the knowing subject. We—the Vienna Circle—neither affirm nor deny any of these theses, but regard them as pseudo-theses, *i.e.,* as void of cognitive meaning. They arise from the use of the material mode, which speaks about "the object," it thereby leads to such pseudo-questions as the "nature of the object," and especially as to whether it is a mere construction or not. The formulation in the formal idiom is as follows: "A physical object-name (*e.g.,* the *word* 'moon') is reducible to sense-data predicates (or perception predicates)."[19]

Or one may treat this as a problem in epistemology as A. J. Ayer and Hans Reichenbach do, for example, when it becomes a matter of the classification of sense data. Certain sense data are delusory or hallucinatory; others are veridical, i.e., consistent and predictable. The former are called subjective rather than objective. The latter are the "real world"—which thus becomes by definition a subclass of the class of sense data. So that objectivity is a property of subjective sense data, not a property of any external world.

Thus Reichenbach says: ". . . the separation of objective and subjective things, within the realm of immediate things, involves an element of arbitrariness; it depends upon what degree of deviation is to be tolerated for an immediate thing which is to be called objective. . . . Our immediate world is, strictly speaking, subjective throughout; it is a substitute world in which we live."[20]

This blending of the objective world into the subjective world, which the positivists perform definitely enough but so deviously as to hide it sometimes even from themselves, is done more explicitly by the pragmatists. Charles Peirce, in a letter to William James about James's doctrine of pure experience, exclaims almost jubilantly: "I also agree with every word you say . . . I have myself preached immediate perception, as you know, and you can't find a place where I distinguish the objective and subjective sides of things."[21] This is a somewhat exaggerated statement. In a calmer tone, Peirce said in a famous definition: "Reality is independent, not necessarily of thought in general, but only of what you or I or any finite number of men may think. . . ."[22]

The subjectivity of the objective world is faced frankly by many scientists. P. W. Bridgman is in the vanguard here. In fact he may even be running a little in front of the front-runners. His position is not only subjectivistic but he has had to defend himself against the charge of being solipsistic. He asserts, for example, that: "My point of view is that science is essentially private, whereas the almost universal counter point of view . . . is that it *must* be public."[23]

Or, in a later book, he says:

Not only is each one of us an individual not able to get away from himself, but the human race as a whole can never get away from itself. . . . When we talk about getting away from ourselves it is we who are talking. . . . The question obtrudes itself "What is this mold of space and time into which our perceptions so inexorably pour the world, and is it a good mold?" Evidence is accumulating that it may not always be a good mold, as when we go so far as we can into the submicroscopic world of quantum phenomena or into the world of supergalaxies. If it is not a good mold, can we invent a better? And even when we have invented it, would it not still be our mold?[24]

Again, Bridgman says: ". . . if one is reconciled to the inevitability of describing the world from himself as center, a unity is thereby automatically restored to the world, the unity conferred by the necessity of seeing everything from a single origin. This is not the illusory unity which we formerly thought we had, but is the only unity we can use, the only unity we need, and the only unity possible in the light of the way things are."[25]

If we consider, then, these two characteristics of the normative epistemologies—that knowledge is prospective and that the external world is infected with a considerable modicum of subjectivity—we may ask what they imply. I know of no significant logical implication from them, but there is a psychological one. The subjectivity found in these empiricisms is primarily the result of the egocentric predicament. This is a psychological, not a logical difficulty. Accordingly the response to it is not a logical but a psychological one. Finding himself thus separated, by virtue of his humanity, from the world about him, the normative empiricist is here faced with his "moment of truth." In dealing with the wave of the future he realizes more acutely than perhaps any philosopher before him the extent to which his world is *his* world and the awe-inspiring degree of his responsibility for it.

Finding himself naked and alone in a situation he never made, the normative empiricist has several alternatives open to him. He might experience a traumatic sensation of revolt or nausea and become an existentialist. He might retreat into mysticism. Or he could face life squarely, accept its challenge, and realize that the fate of his world lies in his own hands for better or for ill.

In Plato's analogy, modern man has come out of the cave, from the shadows into the light of day, and he is blinded by the sudden transition. On the threshold of the unknown he takes stock. What to do? To retreat back into the cave, to be paralyzed and rendered immobile with fear, or to move haltingly and slowly forward out into the mystery?

The final common characteristic of the normative empiricisms is that they all commit the act of faith to move forward. And they do this at a moment in Western civilization when the foreseeable future is fraught with such immediate peril as to require the utmost in courage to be willing to accept responsibility for the decision to move into the unknown. This is an act of faith in themselves and in their fellow men. It is a commitment to the belief that man can accomplish his own salvation. Or that if he cannot accomplish it, he is not worth saving. He may not succeed. He may die. But he will die trying.

Reichenbach says:

> We should not commit the fallacy of believing that the struggle for power is controlled by a superhuman authority that leads it to an ultimately good end;

nor should we commit the complementary fallacy of believing that the good is to be defined as that which is the most powerful. We have seen too many victories of what we regard as immorality, too much success of mediocrity and class egoism. We try to pursue our own volitional ends, not with the fanaticism of the prophet of an absolute truth, but with the firmness of the man who trusts in his own will. We do not know whether we shall reach our aim. Like the problem of a prediction of the future, the problem of moral action cannot be solved by the construction of rules that guarantee success. There are no such rules.[26]

To repeat a passage quoted earlier, William James, in one of the finest paragraphs to come from his pen, described the process of moral growth in human society:

The course of history is nothing but the story of men's struggles from generation to generation to find the more and more inclusive order. *Invent some manner* of realizing your own ideals which will also satisfy the alien demands—that and that only is the path of peace! Following this path, society has shaken itself into one sort of relative equilibrium after another by a series of social discoveries quite analogous to those of science. Polyandry and polygamy and slavery, private warfare and liberty to kill, judicial torture and arbitrary royal power have slowly succumbed to actually aroused complaints; and though some one's ideals are unquestionably the worse off for each improvement, yet a greater total number of them find shelter in our civilized society than in the older savage ways. So far then, and up to date, the casuistic scale is made for the philosopher

already far better than he can make it for himself. . . . And yet if he be a true philosopher he
must see that there is nothing final in any actually
given equilibrium of human ideals, but that, as our
present laws and customs have fought and conquered
other past ones, so they will in their turn be overthrown by any newly discovered order which will
hush up the complaints that they give rise to, without producing others louder still. . . . And although a man always risks much when he breaks
away from established rules and strives to realize
a larger ideal whole than they permit, yet the philosopher must allow that it is at all times open to anyone to make the experiment, provided he fear not to
stake his life and character upon the throw.[27]

NOTES

The following short titles are used in these notes:

Meaning of Truth—*The Meaning of Truth*, William James, 1909.

Pluralistic Universe—*A Pluralistic Universe*, William James, 1909.

Pragmatism—*Pragmatism*, William James, 1907.

Principles—*The Principles of Psychology*, William James, 1890.

Problems—*Some Problems of Philosophy*, William James, 1911.

Radical Empiricism—*Essays in Radical Empiricism*, William James, 1912.

Varieties—*The Varieties of Religious Experience*, William James, 1902.

William James—*The Thought and Character of William James*, Ralph Barton Perry, 1935.

Will to Believe—*The Will to Believe and Other Essays*, William James, 1896.

The quotation on page xi is from *A Pluralistic Universe* by William James.

Chapter 1

1. *William James*, II, 58.
2. *The Literary Remains of the Late Henry James*, edited with an Introduction by William James (Boston: J. R. Osgood and Company, 1885), pp. 158-59.
3. *Ibid.*, pp. 182-86.
4. *Ibid.*, pp. 150-51.
5. *Ibid.*, pp. 59-60.
6. *Varieties*, pp. 160-61. James's son tells us that James is here describing his own experience. See Henry James (ed.), *The Letters of William James* (Boston: Little, Brown, and Company, 1926), I, 145.
7. Henry James, *Substance and Shadow* (Boston: Ticknor and Fields, 1863), p. 155.
8. Henry James, *The Nature of Evil* (New York: Appleton, 1855), p. 51.
9. *William James*, I, 322.
10. *The Atlantic Monthly*, CXLIV (1929), 375.
11. *Will to Believe*, pp. 214-15.
12. *Pluralistic Universe*, p. 311.
13. *William James*, II, 443.

Chapter 2

1. *William James*, II, 25.
2. A contemporary British philosopher, Gilbert Ryle, has called it "the ghost in the machine" theory. See his *The Concept of Mind* (London: Hutchinson, 1949).
3. *Principles*, I, 131.
4. *Principles*, I, 147.
5. *Principles*, I, 130 note.
6. *Principles*, I, 133.

7. *Principles*, I, 145.

8. *Principles*, I, 139.

9. *Principles*, I, 141.

10. *Principles*, I, 159.

11. *Principles*, I, chap. 6.

12. *Principles*, I, 150 ff.

13. *Principles*, I, 149.

14. *Principles*, I, 178-79.

15. *Principles*, I, 343.

16. *Principles*, I, 345.

17. *Principles*, I, 347.

18. *Principles*, I, 288-89.

19. *Will to Believe*, pp. 146 ff.

20. *Will to Believe*, pp. 146-47.

21. *Will to Believe*, pp. 63 ff.

22. *Will to Believe*, p. 11.

23. *Will to Believe*, p. 178.

24. *Will to Believe*, pp. 184 ff.

25. Arthur Eddington, *The Nature of the Physical World* (Cambridge, Eng.: The Cambridge University Press, 1928), pp. xi-xiv.

26. Michael Polanyi, *Personal Knowledge* (Chicago: The University of Chicago Press, 1958), pp. 3-4.

27. Milton K. Munitz, *Space, Time and Creation* (Glencoe, Ill.: The Free Press, 1957), p. 59.

28. P. W. Bridgman, *The Nature of Physical Theory* (Princeton: Princeton University Press, 1936), p. 95.

29. *The Will to Believe*, p. 185.

30. *Principles*, II, 686.

31. *Principles*, II, 676.

32. *Principles*, II, 676.

33. *Principles*, II, 677.

34. *Principles*, II, 678.

35. *Principles*, II, 678.

36. *Principles*, II, 677.

37. *Principles*, II, 677.

38. *Principles*, II, 727.

39. *Principles*, II, 672.

40. *Principles*, II, 672-73.
41. *Principles*, II, 675.
42. *Principles*, II, 669.
43. *Will to Believe*, p. 184.
44. *Principles*, II, 618 note.
45. *Will to Believe*, p. 189.
46. *Will to Believe*, p. 193.
47. *Will to Believe*, p. 194.
48. *Will to Believe*, p. 195.
49. *Will to Believe*, p. 194.
50. *Will to Believe*, p. 195.
51. *Will to Believe*, pp. 202-3.
52. *Will to Believe*, pp. 205-6.
53. *Will to Believe*, pp. 206-8.
54. *Will to Believe*, p. 208.
55. *Will to Believe*, p. 198.
56. *Will to Believe*, pp. 212-13.

Chapter 3

1. William James, "Philosophical Conceptions and Practical Results," *The Journal of Philosophy, Psychology and Scientific Method*, I (1904), 673-75.

2. John Dewey, "The Development of American Pragmatism," in *Studies in the History of Ideas* (New York: Columbia University Press, 1925), II, 364-65.

3. *William James*, II, 450.

4. John Dewey, "An Empirical Survey of Empiricisms," in *Studies in the History of Ideas* (New York: Columbia University Press, 1935), III, 20-21.

5. *William James*, I, 558.

6. *Will to Believe*, pp. 113-14.

7. *Will to Believe*, p. 114.

8. *Pluralistic Universe*, p. 249.

9. *Pragmatism*, pp. 49-50.

10. *Pragmatism*, p. 196.

11. *Pragmatism* p. 198.
12. *Pragmatism*, p. 201.
13. *Pragmatism*, p. 223.
14. *Will to Believe*, p. 209.
15. *Pragmatism*, pp. 222-23.
16. *Pragmatism*, p. 215.
17. *Pragmatism*, p. 257.
18. *Pragmatism*, pp. 76-77.
19. *Pragmatism*, p. 73.
20. *Pragmatism*, p. 233.
21. *Meaning of Truth*, pp. 57-59.
22. *Pragmatism*, p. 247.
23. *Pragmatism*, p. 259.
24. *Pragmatism*, p. 257.
25. *Pragmatism*, p. 217.
26. *Pragmatism*, p. 218.
27. *Pragmatism*, p. 218.
28. *Pragmatism*, p. 218.
29. *Pragmatism*, p. 218.
30. *Pragmatism*, p. 222.
31. *Pragmatism*, pp. 222-24.
32. *Meaning of Truth*, p. xi.
33. See above, note 26 in Chapter II.

Chapter 4

1. *Meaning of Truth*, p. 2.
2. *Meaning of Truth*, pp. 14-15.
3. *Meaning of Truth*, pp. 6-7.
4. *Meaning of Truth*, p. 7.
5. *Meaning of Truth*, p. 41.
6. *Meaning of Truth*, p. 39.
7. *Meaning of Truth*, pp. 39-40.
8. *Meaning of Truth*, p. 18.
9. *Meaning of Truth*, p. 19.
10. *Meaning of Truth*, p. 32.

11. *Meaning of Truth*, p. 37.
12. *Meaning of Truth*, p. 37.
13. *Meaning of Truth*, p. 28.
14. *Meaning of Truth*, p. 143.
15. *Meaning of Truth*, p. 106.
16. *Meaning of Truth*, p. 159.
17. *Meaning of Truth*, p. 237.
18. *Meaning of Truth*, pp. 68-69.
19. *Meaning of Truth*, p. 119.
20. *Meaning of Truth*, p. 100.
21. *Meaning of Truth*. p. 100.
22. *Radical Empiricism*, p. 3.
23. *Meaning of Truth*, p. 49.
24. *Meaning of Truth*, p. 49 note.
25. *Radical Empiricism*, p. 4.
26. *Radical Empiricism*, p. 10.
27. *Radical Empiricism*, p. 107.
28. *Meaning of Truth*, pp. xii-xiii.
29. F. H. Bradley, *Appearance and Reality*, p. 570.
Quoted by James in *Radical Empiricism*, p. 99.
30. *Radical Empiricism*, pp. 113-14.
31. Bradley, *op. cit.*, quoted in *Radical Empiricism*, pp. 111-14.
32. *Pragmatism*, p. 30.
33. *Problems*, p. 40.
34. *Radical Empiricism*, pp. 93-94.
35. *Problems*, p. 148.
36. *Problems*, p. 214.
37. *Pragmatism*, pp. 286 ff.
38. *Pragmatism*, pp. 290-91.
39. *Pragmatism*, p. 300.
40. *Pluralistic Universe*, pp. 309-11.
41. *Radical Empiricism*, p. 194.
42. *Pluralistic Universe*, pp. 309-11.
43. *William James*, II, 443.
44. *Radical Empiricism*, p. 193.
45. *Radical Empiricism*, p. 134.
46. *Radical Empiricism*, p. 80.

47. *Radical Empiricism*, p. 132.

48. *Radical Empiricism*, p. 133.

49. *Principles*, I, 149.

50. *William James*, II, 382.

51. *William James*, II, 444.

52. *Radical Empiricism*, pp. 89-90.

53. William James, *Memories and Studies* (New York: Longmans, Green and Company, 1911), pp. 135-36.

54. *Problems*, p. 221.

55. *Pragmatism*, p. 73.

56. *Problems*, p. 224.

57. *Pluralistic Universe*, pp. 29-30.

Chapter 5

1. *Problems*, p. 221.

2. *Problems*, p. 50.

3. *Problems*, p. 57.

4. *Problems*, p. 79.

5. *Problems*, p. 65.

6. *Principles*, II, 7.

7. Alfred Jules Ayer, *Language, Truth and Logic* (New York: Dover, 1935), p. 101.

8. *Problems*, pp. 59-60.

9. *Pragmatism*, pp. 46-47.

10. Hans Reichenbach, *The Rise of Scientific Philosophy* (Berkeley: University of California Press, 1951), p. 256.

11. P. W. Bridgman, *Reflections of a Physicist* (New York: Philosophical Library, 1950), p. v.

12. *Ibid.* p. 3.

13. Charles S. Peirce, *Collected Papers* (Cambridge, Mass.: Harvard University Press, 1934), V, par. 412.

14. Bridgman, *op. cit.*, p. 32.

15. Reichenbach, *op. cit.*, p. 255.

16. Peirce, *op. cit.*, V, par. 432 and 413.

17. John Dewey, *The Quest for Certainty* (New York: Minton, Balch, 1929), p. 111, note 2.

18. Richard Von Mises, *Positivism* (Cambridge, Mass.: Harvard University Press, 1951), p. 399.

19. Rudolf Carnap, "Testability and Meaning," *Philosophy of Science*, III (1936), 430-31.

20. Hans Reichenbach, *Experience and Prediction* (Chicago: University of Chicago Press, 1938), p. 220.

21. *William James*, II, 433-34.

22. Peirce, *op. cit.*, V, par. 408.

23. Bridgman, *op. cit.*, p. 44.

24. P. W. Bridgman, *The Way Things Are* (Cambridge, Mass.: Harvard University Press, 1959), pp. 6-8.

25. *Ibid.*, p. 248.

26. Reichenbach, *Experience and Prediction*, p. 301.

27. *Will to Believe*, pp. 205-6.

BIBLIOGRAPHY

Books by William James:

The Principles of Psychology. New York, 1890.

Psychology, Briefer Course. New York, 1892.

The Will to Believe and Other Essays in Popular Philosophy. New York, 1897.

Human Immortality: Two Supposed Objections to the Doctrine. Boston, 1898.

Talks to Teachers on Psychology: and to Students on Some of Life's Ideals. New York, 1899.

The Varieties of Religious Experience: A Study in Human Nature. New York, 1902.

Pragmatism: A New Name for Some Old Ways of Thinking. New York, 1907.

The Meaning of Truth: A Sequel to "Pragmatism." New York, 1909.

A Pluralistic Universe: Hibbert Lectures on the Present Situation in Philosophy. New York, 1909.

Some Problems of Philosophy: A Beginning of an Introduction to Philosophy. New York, 1911.

Memories and Studies. New York, 1911.

Essays in Radical Empiricism. New York, 1912.

Collected Essays and Reviews. New York, 1920.

Books relating to William James:

JAMES, HENRY (ed.). *The Letters of William James*. Boston: Little, Brown and Company, 1926.
Two volumes of the letters of James, edited by his son, provide useful and interesting insights into James's life and philosophy.

JAMES, WILLIAM (ed.). *The Literary Remains of the Late Henry James*. Boston: J. R. Osgood and Company, 1885.
Writings of William James's father, with a long introduction by the son. The volume throws a good deal of light on the emotional and intellectual background from which William James came.

MOORE, EDWARD C. *American Pragmatism: Peirce, James, and Dewey*. New York: Columbia University Press, 1961.
A study of the elements in the thought of each of the principal exponents of pragmatism in this country. The pragmatic method is discussed in connection with Peirce's notion of reality, James's notion of truth, and Dewey's notion of the good.

PERRY, RALPH BARTON. *The Thought and Character of William James*. 2 vol. Boston: Little, Brown, and Company, 1935.
Probably the most exhaustive study of the life and thought that has ever been attempted of any philosopher. A Pulitzer Prize winning biography of James by one of his students.

WIENER, PHILIP P. *Evolution and the Founders of Pragmatism*. Cambridge, Mass.: Harvard University Press, 1949.
This book relates the development of pragmatism and the influence of Darwinism on six American thinkers in Cambridge, Massachusetts, in the 1860's and 1870's. One of them was William James.

INDEX

A

Absolute, 137. *See also* God

Activism, 163

Agassiz, Louis, 12

Agnosticism, in the decision-making process, 112-13; James' view of, 99

Ambulation, 133

American Psychological Association, 130

Appearance and Reality, 137, 138

Argument from design, 14-16, 18

Aristotle, 2, 17, 78, 163, 164, 168

Atoms, 28

Augustine, St., 2, 22

Automaton, 41

Ayer, A. J., 173

B

Back-door theory, 56

Bacon, Francis, 164

Behavior, and true ideas, 111; James' orientation toward, 85-86; normative, 42; organic, 42; processes, 110

Belief, 98, 99

Berkeley, George, 117-18, 144; difference from James' views, 144

"Block-universe," *See* Universe

Bohr, Nils, 96

Bradley, F. H., 137, 138

Bridgman, P. W., 54-55, 169, 170, 171, 172; on subjectivity of the objective world, 174-75

C

Calvin, John, 2, 8

Calvinism, 4, 19, 22, 23, 159; effect on James family of, 7-8; New England type, 22

Carnap, 173

Causality, principle of, 45

Causation, 34

Christ, Henry James the elder on, 5